Financial Planning Insights

*Insights Gained from Two Decades
as a Financial Planner*

Dr. Chase W. Armer, CFP®, CFA, EA

Edited by: Daryl W. Wong, CFP®, EA

Financial Planning Insights: Insights gained from two decades as a financial planner

ISBN 978-1-09830-627-4

This book is dedicated to my children, Trevor and Kira. May the insights that I have learned during my career help you to make thoughtful and prudent financial decisions throughout your lives.

This book is also dedicated to the Planned Solutions Team. Many of these insights are the result of working with a smart and talented group of individuals. Your support has nurtured my professional growth. Your dedication to your careers has inspired me to push harder and go further. Our discussions, debates, and interactions have forced me to rethink assumptions, question the validity of financial theories, and strive to bring new and independent thinking to the financial planning process.

Table of Contents

Introduction 7

1. The Secret to Becoming Wealthy 10

2. Planning Priorities and Dilemmas 16

3. Choosing the Right Route 22

4. Why Work 26

5. The Way to Wealth 29

6. Financial Strengths and Weaknesses 32

7. Ranked Spending Approach 37

8. Approaches to Budgeting 41

9. Fixed v. Variable Expenses 51

10. Household Inflation Rate 56

11. What is the Real Cost 62

12. Phantom Debt 66

13. The Next Best Alternative Standard 71

14. Cycles 75

15. The Debt Cycle 84

16. The Asymmetry of Wealth Creation 90

17. Planning Assumptions 96

18. Probabilities and the Unexpected 99

19. Extrapolation, Contrarianism, & Analysis... 104

20. Wealth Equation 108

21. The Often Irrational Nature of Prices............ 112

22. Prices, Values, and Volatility 117

23. Mosaic Approach 122

24. Three Aspects to Risk..................................... 128

25. Risk Minimization v. Risk Maximization...... 134

26. Avoid Financial Ruin....................................... 138

27. Contingency Planning 144

28. Risk Variation.. 149

29. Losses vs. Missed Profits................................ 153

30. Consolidate Gains.. 156

31. Interest Rates and Bond Returns.................... 160

32. Borrowing on the Future................................ 164

33. The Chicken and the Hog................................ 170

34. Real Assets vs. Paper Assets 176

35. Price to Rents Ratio.. 180

36. A Home is Not an Investment 184

37. Selling Liquidity Too Cheap 187

38. Roth v. Traditional.................................... 193

39. Tax Bracket Planning................................ 200

40. Managing Tax Deductions................................ 205

41. Retirement Savings Debt................................ 208

42. Challenges to Early Retirement........................ 211

43. Aggressively Saving for Retirement 215

44. Social Security................................ 218

45. Mortgage Insights................................ 222

46. Planning for Cognitive Decline........................ 227

47. Who Gets What................................ 230

48. Skin in the Game 234

49. Trust but Verify 237

50. Hire a Financial Planner 240

Appendix I................................ 244

About the Author................................ 251

Introduction

F ew truly insightful financial planning tips can be found in a textbook, newspaper, or magazine. They come from years of dealing with real financial issues and working with real people to tackle life's financial and non-financial challenges. Often there is more to financial planning than cash inflows and outflows, taxable income and tax deductions, or investment risk and return. Financial planning decisions have real life implications which go beyond the neat financial models, endless spreadsheets, and advanced math that are used to plan an individual's financial future.

Behavioral finance, the merging of finance and psychology, has shown that many of the ways we have been going about financial planning is all wrong. People are not the rational decision makers that the financial theories assume. Instead people respond to a variety of internal and external factors that influence their hopes and fears, actions and inaction, and ultimately their successes and failures. These factors cannot be captured by an algorithm or any other one-size-fits-all approach to financial planning. They also should not be ignored.

The excessive certainty implied in financial models combined with the seemingly irrational behavior exhibited by real people has led many individuals and financial planners to develop strategies that provide too little margin for error. This lack of margin for error has resulted in reduced financial flexibility when flexibility is needed most, larger losses than the models predicted and that investors could live with, and a general overconfidence that puts too little emphasis on the many financial risks that stalk individuals as they plan for their financial future.

In finance there is great value to being a skeptic. The saying: "If it seems too good to be true it probably is" rings true economic cycle after economic cycle and market cycle after market cycle. It pays to question assumptions, ask what you might be missing, and engage in independent thinking. Contrarian thinking, the willingness to deviate from the herd, can also pay dividends. After all, when it comes to personal finance, common sense is not all that common as emotion often takes over when a cool-headed, rational approach is needed most.

There is some merit to planning for the worst while hoping for the best. The best time to address financial risks is before they are evident. After all, the only useful financial plan is one that can guide an individual through the good times as well as the bad times. There are too many instances where one negative event can do irreparable damage to an individual's finances. Therefore, the first priority should be to identify risks and take action to mitigate them. A good risk management plan that can survive the bad times is the key to a successful financial plan.

This world view is at the core of this book. As a result many of the insights in this book reflect a conservative approach to financial planning. They may be counter to some conventional wisdom which is designed to appeal to people's naturally optimistic nature. However, it is important to stress that these insights do not come from a pessimistic view of the future but rather a more realistic view of the real-life financial challenges that individuals face. After decades of helping real people solve real life financial challenges patterns emerge. When some of these patterns are examined more closely they lead to insights as to how individuals can better think about their finances in order to increase their probability of achieving their goals.

Many of the insights in this book will be applicable to some people and not to others. They may represent a different perspective to a common financial planning dilemma or a rebuke of the accepted theories on how individuals should plan for their future. In many cases they are not backed by scientific research or published studies. These insights are the result of real-life experiences, failures and successes, and the pursuit of financial planning wisdom to augment traditional financial planning knowledge.

The goal of this book is not to persuade but rather to offer a different point of view. Hopefully these insights will spark some debate, inspire new perspectives, and perhaps lead to the discovery of even more insights that can be used to help individuals create, pursue, monitor, and eventually achieve their financial goals.

1

The Secret to Becoming Wealthy

T he secret to becoming wealthy is that there is no secret. There are no special investments that only the wealthy know about. In fact, many of the wealthiest people own large amounts of stocks, bonds, and other publicly available investments. There are no special tax provisions that the wealthy use to avoid paying taxes. In fact, the wealthiest Americans pay the bulk of the taxes in any given year. And there is no one-size-fits-all approach to accumulating wealth. Millions of people have become wealthy using a thousand different strategies. However, there are principles that, combined with a diligent work ethic, financial discipline, and a desire to be financially successful, can lead to wealth.

Principle 1: Focus on the whole picture. When it comes to accumulating wealth the focus naturally gravitates to investment returns. Everyone wants to get the best return that they can so they search far and wide for investments that will lead to wealth. This causes some to fall into too-good-to-be-true investment schemes which often result in ruin. Some chase manias and bubbles in an attempt to capture the high returns but fail to sell before the eventual collapse. Still others follow the hot tips that are passed around which usually prove to not be all that hot. The problem is that the focus on investment returns is only looking at part of the picture. Sure, investment returns are important, but they are only one factor in the wealth creation process. After all, if only a small amount of money is invested in a great investment it may result in a nice increase in value but is unlikely to result in real wealth. Only the lottery can turn a small amount of money into a fortune and those odds are not very good. So, the first step is to save. For most people the largest contributor to their total wealth will be their savings rate. A high savings rate combined with regular contributions to investment accounts and the reinvestment of gains can lead to a large amount of wealth even if the investment returns are less than stellar. Large investment contributions combined with good returns and a sufficient time horizon can lead to significant wealth. Most importantly, investment returns are largely beyond an individual's control whereas they can determine their savings rate and the amount contributed to investments. So when focusing on the whole picture it is clear that saving and investing should take priority over chasing high returns.

Principle 2: Create a legacy. Too often a financial windfall, such as an inheritance, is squandered. People have a tendency to treat money that they earned and saved differently than money that was bestowed on them. The curse of the lottery, where people win millions only to end up broke is a good example. Meanwhile, wealthy people tend to view themselves as stewards of their money with the responsibility to use it wisely and then pass it on to charity or the next generation. Money is a tool. When used intelligently it can build great things. When used poorly it can lead to pain and misery. A key to amassing wealth is to capitalize on financial windfalls by protecting, preserving, and growing the money over time while taking reasonable distributions as compensation for diligent management and oversight. This will create a legacy of wealth that can last for a lifetime and beyond.

Principle 3: It takes flexibility. There is a common misconception that the wealthy are able to employ tax professionals to find loopholes that allow them to avoid paying taxes. In reality, tax statistics show that the wealthiest 10% of American taxpayers pay over 70% of the total income tax. So clearly the wealthy are not able to legally avoid paying taxes. However, there is truth to the belief that many wealthy people do engage in tax planning to reduce their tax liability. After all, there are many ways that an individual can legally reduce their taxes by arranging their financial affairs in a way that results in less tax owed. However, this process is less about being able to afford to hire a team of tax consultants and more about having the financial flexibility to be able to shift financial resources to be more tax efficient.

For example, having sufficient financial flexibility to be able to set money aside into long-term investment vehicles, such as retirement accounts, can create tax benefits. The ability to deduct contributions, tax-deferred or tax-free growth, and the ability to determine the timing of distributions are all byproducts of such a strategy. However, retirement accounts are often subject to penalties if the money is withdrawn before retirement. Therefore, an individual must have the financial flexibility to be able to set money aside for years or decades without needing to access it. Illiquid investments, such as real estate, can also be tax efficient when properly incorporated into an investment and tax plan. However, buying real estate requires a substantial down payment, good credit, and sufficient discretionary income to be able to cover periods of negative cash flow (periods when the property is not rented or the owner must pay for repairs). In other words, it requires financial flexibility that comes from a high savings rate and discretionary income. Finally, at times intelligent tax planning may actually result in prepaying taxes at a lower tax rate in order to avoid paying taxes in the future at a higher tax rate. Often the tax payments must come from savings so it is necessary to have sufficient savings to be able to engage in such a strategy. The flexibility offered by a high savings rate and a large nest egg that can be used for tax and investment planning can allow an individual to decrease their tax liability over their lifetime which can be an important contributor to wealth creation.

Principle 4: Think long-term rather than short-term. Too many people want to get rich quick. Yet this is hard to do as it requires significant luck. Meanwhile, it can be quite easy to get rich slowly. All it takes is diligent savings, disciplined investment, and a long-term mindset. There is an old saying that it takes 20 years to become an overnight sensation. Often when we become aware of an individual's success it feels like their success came very quickly. What we don't see is the years of incremental steps that they took to eventually achieve the level of success that gets them noticed. Building wealth works the same way. For most it takes decades of incremental steps that lead to small improvements until eventually it adds up to the accumulation of significant wealth. This is why it is important to focus on the long-term by taking the incremental, get rich slowly, approach to building wealth. This will not only increase the likelihood that an individual will reach their objective but also keep them from getting off track when short-term setbacks occur.

Principle 5: Don't bet the farm. One way to become wealthy is to make high risk and high return bets. However, only a few of the people who implement this strategy will be successful as only a small percentage are statistically likely to win a large number of low probability but high return bets. Meanwhile, those who implement this strategy but are not successful will likely meet financial ruin. The goal should be to have a high probability of becoming wealthy and a low probability of financial ruin.

The goal should be to mitigate the risks of financial ruin while participating in the gains to the greatest degree possible. One of the best ways to do this is to diversify financial resources. This means avoid holding a large amount of employer stock so that household income and assets are not both tied to the performance of one company. It also means holding assets that are not correlated to each other so that they do not tend to increase or decrease in value in response to changes in the same factors. There will be setbacks from time to time. Proper diversification will minimize the impact of those setbacks so that they do not lead to financial distress or force an investor to abandon their longer-term financial plan. It is important to monitor investments so that an asset that performs well does not grow to become too large of a percentage of total wealth. When manias and bubbles take hold of the market those who are disciplined in taking profits may benefit to a lesser degree than others but the negative impact will be less when the trends reverse. Those who let their gains ride so that an investment, or similar group of investments, becomes too large a of percentage of their overall wealth may risk financial ruin.

We often measure wealth in relation to the wealth of others. Not everyone can be in the top 10%, 20%, or 30% in terms of total wealth but that does not mean they cannot achieve financial success. Those who choose to follow these basic principles, as well as the other insights included in this book, will give themselves a good chance of being among those who achieve a comfortable financial life.

2

Planning Priorities and Dilemmas

One of the common planning mistakes that individuals make is to prioritize the wrong goals and objectives over those that are likely to have a greater impact on their financial well-being. Often this comes down to making emotional decisions about how to allocate financial resources or failing to properly weigh the tradeoffs involved which can lead to putting too much emphasis on factors such as return while giving too little weight to other factors such as risk. Financial planning is a personalized process that is designed to reflect the goals and objectives of the individual. However, it is important for individuals to know the full implications of their decisions ahead of time so that they can properly assess their options. Often with some additional financial education individuals may change their perspective to reflect a more balanced set of priorities and tradeoffs. In other cases, they may choose to proceed with their plan but will have a better understanding of the costs and benefits of their decisions.

For example, individuals often prioritize investing over securing the proper insurance coverage (prioritize potential return over risk mitigation). This strategy reflects the general optimism that many people feel for the future as well as the belief that the risks will not impact them. In reality there is far more that can be lost than gained by prioritizing the allocation of financial resources to investments rather than insurance. If an individual were to become disabled or subject to a liability claim their investment dollars are unlikely to cover the substantial costs of maintaining their lifestyle or covering the liability. Meanwhile, allocating just a portion of free cash flow to insurance premiums can provide a large amount of protection against risks that could result in financial ruin.

At each stage of the financial planning process an emphasis should be put on consolidating and protecting gains by mitigating the risks that can lead to a major financial set back. As an individual's financial resources increase the amount of protection should keep pace. If insurance coverage is not a priority the money allocated to investments as well as other assets may be at risk possibly forcing the individual to start over. Sufficient insurance coverage, as well as the use of other risk management strategies, should be a top priority in any financial plan. Otherwise, the time and money invested in improving one's situation may be wasted and they may end up worse off than they were at the start.

Another common mistake is prioritizing compensation over employee benefits. Studies have shown that individuals value their employee benefits at roughly half the actual cost of those benefits. Therefore, they would choose to forgo their employee benefits if they saw just half of the cost of those benefits added to their paycheck. Yet employee benefits can be an important part of a financial plan and can come with benefits above and beyond those of additional compensation. For example, employer provided health insurance is a common employee benefit which often can be purchased at a lower cost than private insurance due to the group nature of employer policies. In addition, employer paid health insurance is tax-free whereas most people are unable to deduct all the cost of private health insurance on their income taxes due to limits on the deductibility of medical expenses. In addition, many employers offer Flexible Spending Accounts (FSAs) or Health Savings Accounts (HSAs) which allow employees to allocate money each year to health care costs on a tax-free basis. These plans can result in substantial tax savings but too few employees use them or do not use them to their full potential.

Retirement benefits, whether in the form of a pension plan or matching contributions to an employer sponsored retirement plan, can also be of substantial value. Yet these benefits are too often undervalued because the benefit is not realized until far into the future. Retirement benefits can also be very tax efficient as they often transfer compensation that would be taxed at the individual's highest tax rate while they are working to income in retirement which may be taxed at a lower average tax rate. The long-term value of these benefits can be substantial and therefore should not be ignored when weighing employment options and compensation packages.

There are also benefits such as stock options and restricted stock that can be a valuable addition to an employee's retirement savings plan or investment plan. These plans are often complex and have an uncertain future value but should not be overlooked due to the substantial value that they may offer.

In addition, a number of other employee benefits allow employees to shift a portion of their compensation from taxable income to tax-free benefits. These include parking and transportation benefits, employee wellness programs, child and dependent care benefits, and employee education and training programs among others.

Individuals also often prioritize personal assets over investment assets. For example, many people will "invest" their money in a larger, more valuable home with the belief that the home appreciation will be used to fund their long-term financial goals. The problem with allocating money to personal assets is that the individual's standard of living increases in-line with the value of the asset (see A Home is not an Investment). The only way to benefit from the appreciation is to sell the home and to downsize which generally requires some sacrifice in terms of the individual's standard of living (moving to a smaller, less costly home) or their housing choices (moving to a lower cost of living location). The same is true of investing in a vacation home. Vacation home ownership generally offsets other vacation expenses but also comes with additional expenses to maintain the home. Unless it is rented to generate income, the costs are likely to be greater than the benefits. In addition, the vacation home must be sold to cash-out the value. Once the home is sold the owner may need to allocate the money to future vacation expenses to maintain their previous standard of living.

Meanwhile, traditional investments, such as stocks, bonds, etc., may appreciate in value and/or generate income with the gains reinvested for the future without impacting an individual's standard of living. When these assets increase in value they represent a net gain that can be used to fund future retirement expenses or other goals.

Some people also prioritize college funding over retirement funding. Choosing a college for a child can be an emotional decision as everyone wants the best for their children but the cost of a top-tier college education can be unaffordable for many. In addition, there is no guarantee that a college education will pay off in the form of higher earnings for the child. In fact, in the last recession many college graduates were unable to find meaningful employment and were forced to move back in with their parents after graduation. Meanwhile, most people have a limited number of working years to fund retirement. If they put their financial resources into college education expenses rather than retirement funding both they and their child may end up with no financial safety net.

On the other hand, if financial resources are allocated to retirement the child may still be able to fund their education through loans. This will keep the family safety net in-tact while the college costs can be paid off over time. Limiting the resources that are allocated to college to that which the parent or guardian can afford also may force some discipline into college selection and funding decisions. If the parent finds that they end up with sufficient assets to fund retirement they can always help their child to pay off their student loans after the fact.

Finally, too often people prioritize other financial planning issues over estate planning. The failure to set up an estate plan can be a costly mistake as the time and cost of settling an estate plan through the courts can far exceed the cost of an estate plan. People often justify their decision to avoid estate planning based on the theory that it will not affect them because by the time an estate plan is needed they will be dead. The flaw in this logic is that an estate plan is not just used after an individual dies; it also comes into play when an individual becomes incapacitated. In this case, the estate planning documents determine who will make medical decisions, manage finances, and determine living arrangements. In addition, when there is a minor child involved the estate planning documents may determine who will have custody of the child and control the assets that are set aside for the child's care. For most people these are important decisions which they would prefer to make themselves rather than leave them up to the courts to decide. For this reason, an estate plan should be a high financial planning priority for just about everyone.

Financial priorities can differ from person to person which is part of what makes financial planning a unique and dynamic process. It is important that people not put too much emphasis on short-term financial goals without first considering the longer-term implications that those decisions may have. Financial planning is about taking a long-term perspective to achieve financial goals and objectives while mitigating the risks that can cause the plan to fail.

3

Choosing the Right Route

Financial planning is similar to preparing for a long journey. The financial plan is the map for the journey. So, the first steps are for an individual to figure out where they are on the map and determine their desired destination. Figuring out the starting point on the map is typically a part of the data gathering process in which a financial planner gathers records of the individual's income and expenses, assets and liabilities, and financial resources and obligations. This creates a picture of the individual's current financial status in relation to their age, standard of living, and financial responsibilities.

The desired destination is a reflection of the individual's financial goals. It may be that they want to retire comfortably, fund their children's education, or buy a vacation home. The destination will be different for everyone depending on their goals, dreams, and priorities. The key is to quantify the goals to determine the exact coordinates on the map that marks the desired destination. In addition, quantifiable goals make it possible to track the progress toward goals and know when the destination is near.

Once the starting point, or the "you are here" point, is determined and the desired financial destination is quantified the next step is to decide the route that will be taken from the starting point to the end point. Often there are many different routes that one can choose from. This is similar to selecting a GPS route when planning for a long road trip. Some of the routes may be shorter but exposed to greater risks. For example, there may be sharp turns or no center median to protect against the mistakes of other drivers. Other routes may be labelled as faster but the roads will be congested with many drivers travelling at high speeds so that an accident can lead to a major pile-up and significant delays. Still other routes may be longer and slower but offer the driver a less stressful and more enjoyable journey.

It is important that individuals choose the route that is the right fit for them. Often one of the largest mistakes people make when engaging in financial planning is choosing the wrong route. For example, some may have delayed starting their journey and find that it may be difficult to reach their desired destination within their desired time frame. In an attempt to make up for lost time they choose the fastest route and take big risks by driving at a high speed. The problem with this approach is that a wrong move can lead to a major setback. For example, many people have found themselves in difficult financial situations after investing too heavily in technology stocks, commodities, real estate, etc. during boom periods in an attempt to make up for lost time only to see their financial resources greatly reduced during the following bust.

Another common mistake is choosing a shortcut. There are always shortcuts that look attractive to those who are not knowledgeable about the financial road conditions. People take these shortcuts often wonder why others do not see the obvious advantages that they present. However, these shortcuts come with their own set of risks, such as road closures or expensive tolls. In some cases, while the road appears on the map it actually doesn't exist. Therefore, time and money are spent making very little progress as the route that appeared to be an advantageous shortcut was actually too good to be true.

Then there is the route that appears shorter but may be far riskier than the individual can handle. Even if the risk does not lead to a financial disaster it could cause the driver to rethink the journey. For example, a route that is too risky could cause an individual to delay saving and investing for the future because they fear the volatility of the financial markets, distrust banks and other financial institutions, and worry that their money will not buy as much in the future as it can today. These may be valid fears, but it is far riskier to avoid saving for the future than it is to brave the uncertainty that is a part of financial planning. Those that are risk adverse should choose a route with few risks even if that means the journey will take longer.

Another risk from choosing the wrong route is that an individual may be tempted to turn back when the road conditions deteriorate. Turning back at the wrong time, which is akin to selling risky investments after a sharp decline in value, can cost an individual precious time which is an important factor when planning a road trip or engaging in long-term financial planning. Therefore, it is important to choose a route that will minimize the risk that the traveler will choose to turn back at an inopportune time and therefore extend their journey or make it impossible for them to reach their desired destination altogether.

A good guide knows that the time spent planning a journey is an important key to making it to the destination safely and on schedule. A good financial planner knows that creating a financial plan is an important key to helping their clients increase the probability of achieving their financial goals within a reasonable time frame. A financial decision can only be as good as the financial plan that guides it. A financial journey without a plan is similar to a road trip without a map or GPS, the probability of reaching the desired destination is low and even those who do reach their goal will likely take much longer to do so.

4

Why Work

Work plays a central role in many people's lives. Most people spend roughly a quarter of their time working. For some this is more time than they spend doing anything else, including sleeping and spending time with family. This is a major commitment of one of life's most valuable resources: time. So why do people do it? Why to people work?

Most people work for one of two reasons. The first is to benefit others by producing the goods and services that they want or need and the corresponding feelings of responsibility, pride, and accomplishment that come with it. The second is to benefit themselves by earning the money and benefits needed to cover the expenses of today and possibly plan for the future. Of course, those who are lucky are motivated by both. There are ways to become one of these lucky people through long-term planning, an understanding of economics, and financial discipline.

It is important to understand the most valuable financial resource that most people possess is their labor (the ability to do work for compensation). Economists call this human capital. An individual's human capital is the value of their lifetime earnings from working. As an individual spends time working, they turn their human capital into financial capital (money) which they can spend or save. Therefore, a special emphasis should be put on maximizing the value of human capital.

The first and most obvious way that an individual can increase the value of their human capital is to invest in education and job skills. Generally, but not always, the more education and job skills someone possesses the higher their earnings potential over their lifetime. Of course, the benefit of the higher earnings potential should be weighed against the cost of securing the education and job skills as well as the risk that the expected increase in earnings may not materialize.

A second, and often overlooked, part of human capital is motivation. There are a lot of ways to earn money. It is important to choose one that produces a sense of excitement to do the work and a feeling of satisfaction for a job well done. After all, someone who is motivated by their work is more likely to do their job well and therefore may be able to capture greater earnings over their lifetime. This quality can often lead to as much financial success as formal education or training programs.

It is also important to properly value employee benefits. The value of insurance benefits; such as health insurance, life insurance, disability insurance, etc.; as well as retirement benefits and other employee benefits may be a significant portion of the total value of a worker's human capital. Therefore, taking steps to maximize the value of these benefits is an important part of maximizing the value of human capital.

Another factor is the impact that excessive debt can have on human capital and motivation. Paying excessive amounts in interest means less human capital is available for spending or saving. Therefore, it is important to be careful to limit the use of debt so that excess human capital (wages less spending) can be saved rather than used to pay interest on past purchases. In addition, high debts can reduce the motivation to work. If the financial benefit from work goes to creditors rather than funding spending or long-term financial goals it can sap the motivation to work.

Lastly, it is important to be disciplined in converting human capital into financial capital. Time is the most valuable resource. Every day that is worked cannot be repeated. If that time is converted into progress toward long-term financial goals it can create the motivation to excel at work. On the other hand, a lack of progress on financial goals can make work feel like running on a treadmill: a lot of effort with no movement in the desired direction.

Given the amount of time most people spend working, it is important to maximize the benefits from work. This means viewing work and the income that it produces as a critical financial resource that needs to be managed carefully. For most people, long-term financial success will require putting as much effort into managing their human capital as they put into managing their financial capital.

5

The Way to Wealth

ecoming wealthy is something that is obtainable by just about everyone. The problem is that it requires three things that most people are not willing to do. These are hard work, a willingness to delay rewards, and a willingness to take risks. Each of these may appear simple on the surface but they are easier said than done. In addition, many people may be able to follow one or two of these steps but it takes all three to have a high probability of success.

Many people can be admired for working hard. There are people in every profession at a variety of levels of compensation who put in long hours and diligently work at their chosen craft. However, for many the motivation for hard work is the short-term gratification of increased material wealth. In many cases, the rate of a worker's spending outpaces their level of earnings. This leads to consumer debt which means a large portion of the fruits of their labor goes to interest payments. In this example hard work may lead to the semblance of wealth in the form of personal assets and a high standard of living but not real wealth.

In addition, many people work hard but are not willing to take risks with their careers. They are content to work on the front lines but do not want to take on the added responsibility, stress, and professional growth that is required to advance their careers. Moving beyond one's comfort zone is not easy. It requires constant professional development, advancing skills, and increasing responsibility with no guarantee that it will pay off. In other words, it takes a willingness to take risks by investing time, money, and energy in an endeavor that may not be rewarded. This aversion to risk may prevent them from getting the most out of their earnings potential during their working years. They may fear that if they attempt to advance their career they may fail and lose the job security that they feel in their current position. So, they stay put choosing security over increased compensation.

There are those who are very good at delaying rewards by diligently saving for the future. They save effectively because they place a high value on financial security. For this reason, they are not willing to put their savings at risk. So, they are unwilling to invest their savings in a way that will allow it to grow from a nice nest egg into real wealth.

Of course, there are also people who are willing to take big risks in an attempt to amass wealth. However, they do not incorporate delayed rewards into the equation so they fall for get-rich-quick schemes or count on luck, such as winning the lottery, for a path to wealth. This strategy will work for a very small percentage of those that attempt it but for most it's a fool's errand. In addition, the lucky few who beat the odds and win big but are unwilling to delay rewards often spend lavishly or continue to chase big payoffs and in the process lose the wealth that they temporarily possessed.

For the equation to work all three factors must be included. An individual must be willing to work incredibly hard by putting in the time and effort to make the most that they can from their labor. They must also be willing to take risks and have the self-confidence needed to reach their full potential. For the vast majority of people, earnings from work will be the foundation of their financial success. Therefore, they must take the steps required to get the most out of their hard work.

After hard work comes the discipline to delay rewards by saving a large percentage of what is earned. Instead of borrowing to invest in the future by taking out student loans, large mortgages, or small business loans most people will be better served by saving and investing in themselves.

Finally, accumulating wealth requires taking calculated risks. Most people do not have the earning power to save their way to wealth. They must find a way to grow their savings over time. This requires a willingness to take strategic risks to increase their earning power and their financial wealth. However, it should be stressed that savings is a limited resource so it should only be allocated to risks that have a reasonable expectation for return with a very small chance of financial ruin.

This equation does not guarantee that everyone who uses it will become wealthy. Hard work does not always pay off. In addition, those who save a large percentage of their earnings may find that many short-term financial responsibilities are competing for the use of their savings making it challenging to think about the future. Finally, not all risks pay off. However, those that follow this path will have a higher probability of financial success than those that do not.

6

Financial Strengths and Weaknesses

inancial planning is often about finding a balance between two or more factors. For example, a common budgeting goal is to find a balance between cash inflows and cash outflows. When focusing on investments the goal is often to balance risk and return. With income taxes the goal may be to balance the tax owed and the tax withheld throughout the year. So often financial matters have a yin and yang, a pro and con, or a cost and benefit. Therefore, it should not be surprising that many financial strengths come with a corresponding financial weakness which should be identified and managed. Otherwise the benefit of the positive aspects of a financial plan may be eroded or offset by a risk that was not addressed.

For example, a strength of a financial plan may be high wage income. Someone with high earning power has the benefit of having income at their disposal to fund their spending as well as longer-term financial goals. However, a large amount of earnings can be difficult to replace through savings should the high-earner die or become disabled. Fortunately, life and disability insurance can be used to address this risk. The problem is the higher the earned income the greater the amount of insurance coverage that will generally be needed which can result in high insurance premiums. In addition, it is important that the coverage limits and policy terms are reviewed regularly to make sure the coverage is sufficient and the policies do not lapse before the insured has sufficient savings to replace their earned income. Otherwise a loss of wage income may require a major adjustment to the household's standard of living and long-term financial plans as a high level of earnings is not easily replaced from other income sources.

Similarly, a high level of household income from wages or other sources can be a financial strength. The drawback is that the US tax system primarily focuses on taxing income rather than spending or wealth. So, a high level of household income is likely to result in a large income tax liability. Typically, diligent and consistent tax planning can mitigate but not completely avoid this financial weakness. However, the alternative is to haphazardly pay whatever is due at the end of the year which can lead to thousands more paid in taxes than would otherwise be owed.

Along the same vein, the ability to fund a good standard of living can be a financial strength. However, a high standard of living will require a greater level of wealth accumulation to be able to continue that standard of living in retirement. This can increase the amount of time or money, or both time and money, that it will take to be able to fund retirement goals. In addition, it may increase the risk that the household will not reach the retirement funding objectives by the time they reach their desired retirement age or are forced to retire due to layoffs, medical issues, or other unforeseen circumstances. Fortunately, a retirement plan can determine the retirement savings needed and help to create a balance between the amount of money dedicated to fund current standard of living and the amount of money set aside to fund retirement income.

A large retirement account balance can also be an enviable financial strength. It takes years, if not decades, of diligent savings and disciplined investing to accumulate a large nest egg in an employer sponsored retirement plan or an IRA. In addition, a larger retirement account balance can create the feeling of a stable and comfortable retirement. However, retirement accounts are typically invested directly or indirectly into stocks and bonds making them subject to the volatility of the financial markets. The larger the retirement account balance the greater the dollar losses that are likely to occur when there is a market downturn. In this case, an investment risk management plan may be an effective way to manage the volatility of the financial markets and mitigate the risk of a large drop in value. Even a fairly small percentage decrease on a large balance can result in an uncomfortable loss of value. This could lead to panicked selling or a decision to reduce risk at a bad time making it difficult to recover. A good investment risk management plan may reduce, but not eliminate, this financial weakness.

Holding nonretirement assets of significant value can also be a financial strength. Typically, nonretirement accounts can include a greater variety of investments such as real estate, ownership in a small business, or partnership interests which can lead to greater diversification and lower overall risk. However, unlike many retirement accounts most nonretirement assets are not protected from liability claims. This means that these assets may be at risk from a legal judgement or a claim by creditors. Therefore, liability protection strategies and liability insurance become an important part of a financial plan in order to protect the assets from legal claims.

A pension can be another financial strength in retirement. Often pension income is a good source of diversification of income sources and can lower the overall level of risk in retirement. The problem with pension income is that it typically does not keep up with the general level of prices leading to inflation risk. Should the economy experience several years of high inflation like it did in the late 1970s and early 1980s, the purchasing power of pension income may decline significantly over just a few years. This risk can be offset by investing other retirement resources in assets that are likely to appreciate in value when the rate of inflation is high. This way if the rate of inflation increases the investments should increase in value and can be used to offset some, or all, of the loss of purchasing power.

Large real estate holdings can also be a financial strength. Real estate can produce income in the form of rent or lease payments and may appreciate in value over time. The problem is that real estate cannot be quickly converted into cash. Small portions of a structure cannot be sold to generate cash and real estate commissions can make it costly to sell, not to mention the possible negative tax implications from selling real estate. It may be possible to borrow the equity out of real estate holdings but the required payments on the debt will offset all or a portion of the income the real estate generates. In addition, there are periods when real estate produces negative cash flow as the expenses must still be paid when the property is not rented. Therefore, it is important to mitigate this risk by holding sufficient reserves in assets that can be quickly and easily converted into cash. This will protect the real estate owner from the risk of borrowing on unfavorable terms or being forced to sell at an inopportune time.

A large amount of wealth is perhaps the ultimate financial strength, yet even this comes with its own challenges. For example, those with significant wealth may be subject to the estate tax when they die. Estate tax (sometimes called a wealth tax or death tax) is a separate tax that may be paid by the estate of the wealthy after they die. While the estate tax only affects the very wealthy the amount that exceeds the exemption equivalent credit is taxed at a very high rate. This can be a major problem for those whose wealth is concentrated in illiquid and difficult to sell assets such as a privately held business or real estate. In some cases, life insurance can mitigate this risk by providing the liquidity needed to pay the estate tax after the owner's death. In other cases, the owner may be able to reduce this financial weakness by entering into an agreement to sell all or a portion of their holdings at their death to generate the money needed to pay the estate tax.

Given that financial strengths have corresponding financial weaknesses it is important to maximize the strengths while mitigating the weaknesses. The first step to mitigating weaknesses is to identify them. The next step is to take action to avoid, transfer, or hedge the risk.

7

Ranked Spending Approach

Part of a financial planner's job is to take complex ideas and simplify them so they are easily understandable. This is especially important when working with young people who are starting to plan their financial lives. They are finally making money and they want to be smart with it but don't know where to start. Sure, they have long-term dreams of buying a home, maybe having children, and retiring one day but those things all seem far off in the future. They want to know how they should get started, which goals should be prioritized, and if there is a simple framework they can use to understand and plan their finances.

So where should they start? Perhaps insurance is the best place to start. Protect what they have before attempting to improve their situation. On the other hand, if they have high earnings maybe tax planning is the place to start. Then again, starting to save for retirement at a young age can be beneficial as the savings have more time to grow and compound.

There is no one right answer. However, there is a simple philosophy that can be used called the Ranked Spending Approach. People are busy so it is important to focus their financial planning time and effort on the areas that are likely to have the largest impact on their financial life. Using this principle, the Ranked Spending Approach targets financial planning issues in the order of the largest cost to the smallest cost over a person's lifetime. It starts with "The Big Five" spending categories in the following order:

1. Taxes

2. Retirement

3. Housing

4. Insurance

5. Education

Taxes take many different forms which combined take a large bite out of the average person's lifetime income. Most people focus on income taxes but employment taxes (Social Security and Medicare taxes), sales tax, property tax, and many other smaller taxes add up to make this the most expensive spending category for many households. Therefore, taxes can be a great place to start when attempting to devise strategies to use a household's finances as efficiently as possible. After all, even a small percentage improvement in the largest spending category is likely to yield a greater benefit than a large percentage change in a small spending category.

Retirement may feel like it is a long way out for someone who is just starting their financial journey. But retirement is such a large expense it is important to start early to make it manageable. Starting early allows an individual to take advantage of a greater number of years to save and grow their investments, gain years of pension service, and/or earn Social Security credits. In addition, when retirement savings is incorporated into a tax plan it can be used to reduce the current or future tax burden. For this reason, it is advisable to create a retirement plan after the tax plan while coordinating the two.

A house can be a good investment for the future or a financial burden. The difference hinges on the affordability of the home. Too often young people make purchasing a home their top priority. They also may overextend themselves financially by purchasing a home they cannot afford. This forces them to delay funding other financial goals as they struggle to make oversized mortgage payments, pay property taxes, and fund other upkeep costs. Purchasing a home is often the largest single purchase an individual will make so it is important that it is coordinated with the tax plan (mortgage interest and property taxes may be tax deductible) and the retirement plan (housing costs in retirement are an important part of modeling retirement spending). If a home purchase will require the sacrifice of other long-term goals it may be advisable to rent rather than overpay for a home which may become a financial burden.

Insurance costs include the premiums paid for homeowners/renters insurance, auto insurance, life and disability insurance, and health insurance. Taken together, whether paid out-of-pocket, through a mortgage escrow account, or an employer paid benefit package, these premiums can add up to a large sum each year. Therefore, it is important to be sufficiently insured while allocating insurance premiums as efficiently as possible. This requires identifying potential risks, determining which risks to insure and which to retain, and then creating a risk management plan that provides sufficient coverage at a reasonable cost.

Education costs can be substantial for those who choose to fund them. The cost of attending college as well as trade schools have increased at a faster pace than inflation over the past several decades and show little signs of slowing. At the same time the income differential between those who have a college degree or specialized training and those who do not has increased making higher education a worthwhile investment for many. However, the explosion of student loan debt, as well as the high interest rates on student loans, has become a burden for many young people. This puts them in the difficult situation of planning to pay off their own student loan debt while also wanting to plan to help fund their children's higher education expenses. For this reason, education planning should be incorporated into a tax plan (some education expenses may be tax deductible), retirement plan (do not prioritize dependent's education over retirement goals), and housing plan (overpaying for a home can limit the ability to pay education expenses).

Tackling "The Big Five" spending categories will put most people on the path to financial success. Those who choose to be more comprehensive can then address the many smaller spending categories in an effort to make further gains. However, it is most important to first establish a strong financial foundation before addressing the smaller spending categories that comprise day-to-day standard of living.

8

Approaches to Budgeting

L et's face it, almost no one likes budgeting. After all, budgeting is the process of putting constraints on a household's finances and most people do not like constraints. However, budgeting is an important part of tracking a household's finances and making progress toward financial goals. Fortunately, there arc ways to make the budgeting process less miserable. One is to find the approach to budgeting that is the best fit. In this way, creating a budget is like buying a new shirt. If the shirt is too rigid it will feel uncomfortable and likely will not be worn very often. However, if the shirt is flexible in the right places it will feel better and therefore will be more likely to be worn more often. So, the first goal of budgeting should be to find a budgeting approach that is the right fit so that it is not too uncomfortable and is actually used.

Incremental Approach:

The incremental approach involves analyzing past spending to create a baseline for the amount allocated to key spending categories. For example, a spreadsheet or other software programs can be used to categorize a household's spending over the past six months and derive the average monthly amount spent on each category. This is the starting point for creating spending targets. Then, as the name implies, the incremental approach involves making small adjustments to the spending targets to bring them more in-line with economic reality, personal values, and preferences. This may also be an opportunity to target lower spending in a given category, or categories, to free up cash flow which can be saved for longer-term goals such as retirement. Typically, this is an interactive process in which small adjustments are made to spending targets in order to slowly change spending habits and move closer to achieving longer-term goals. The benefit of this approach is that the change is gradual, so it does not feel as restrictive or painful as making big changes to spending patterns all at once. The downside is that it can be easy to revert to old habits if the adjustments are too small and therefore are not taken seriously. In addition, if major spending changes are needed to get on track to achieve long-term financial goals then the progress using the incremental approach may be too slow to play catch-up.

Household Spending Benchmarking Approach:

Household spending benchmarking involves using average household spending data to create a target for each budget category. For example, a household can determine their annual after-tax income and then apply a percentage of that income to different budget categories to determine the target spending amount for the category. This creates a benchmark, or measuring stick, by which spending can be analyzed and adjusted to create a reasonable budget.

The average household spending published by the US Bureau of Labor Statistics (BLS) can be a good jumping off point. The BLS publishes the average household spending for several major spending categories which can be used to assess how spending patterns are similar or differ from the average.

Average Household Spending

Category	Spending Target
Housing (Rent or Mortgage, Real Estate Taxes, Insurance, Maintenance, and Utilities)	25.3%
Transportation (Auto Payment, Insurance, Registration, Fuel, and Maintenance)	12.1%
Food and Dining (In-home Meals and Dining Out)	9.7%
Medical (Insurance Premiums, Co-Payments, Prescriptions, Etc.)	6.2%
Recreation (Entertainment, Vacations, Dependent's Extra Curricular Activities)	3.9%
Shopping (Clothing, Personal Care Items, Gifts, Etc.)	2.4%
Insurance (Social Security, Medicare, Life Insurance, Disability Insurance, etc.)	8.7%
Other (Miscellaneous Spending not included in other categories)	8.5%

Savings (Retirement Savings, Emergency Fund, and Saving for Large Purchases)	23.2%

Source: US Bureau of Labor Statistics

For example, a household with after tax income of $6,250 per month would expect to spend $1,562.50 on housing, $756.25 on transportation, and $606.25 on food and dining each month. The benefit of using the household spending benchmarking approach is that the targets are based on real numbers rather than past data or an arbitrary estimate of a reasonable spending target for each category. The drawback is that no household is truly average. Every household is unique and therefore the spending averages may vary based on the region of the country, size of the household, annual income, etc.

It is important to maintain flexibility when creating a budget. Therefore, the household spending benchmark is just a jumping off point. Once the initial targets are created they should be tweaked, increasing one category while decreasing another, so that the final spending targets reflect the real-life factors that influence the household's spending. When looking for areas where spending can be cut to increase saving it is best to start with the largest spending categories. Even a small percentage change in a large spending category can free-up a sizable sum to allocate elsewhere or add to saving (see Ranked Spending Approach). It should also be noted that there is no money allocated to debt payments other than a home mortgage included in housing and possibly an auto loan payment included in transportation. Therefore, credit card payments, student loan payments, and personal loan payments will likely have to come out of the savings category. This can make debt a real budget-buster as it can greatly reduce the amount that can be allocated to long-term financial goals.

Discretionary Cash Flow Approach:

The discretionary cash flow approach ignores the spending categories used in the previous two approaches to budgeting. Instead it takes a macro view to determine the amount of money available for day-to-day spending after all obligations and goals are funded. This is the most flexible approach as the discretionary cash flow can be spent in any way while still putting limits on the overall spending.

The discretionary cash flow approach starts with the total of all sources of pretax income. This can be wages, self-employment income, retirement income, etc. Then nondiscretionary expenses such as debt payments, income taxes, payroll taxes, etc. are subtracted. After that the target savings amount needed to achieve long-term financial goals, such as retirement, are subtracted as well as the amounts that must be set aside to fund expenses that occur on an irregular schedule, such as real estate taxes, insurance premiums, and an emergency fund. What is left is the amount that is available to be spent without defaulting on an obligation to the government or creditors and without failing to fund financial goals. It can be useful to convert this number into a monthly amount to determine the target spending amount per month. At this point there are no categories or arbitrary restrictions on how the money can be spent as long as total spending does not exceed the amount of discretionary cash flow.

The benefit of this approach is that it is less standardized and therefore can be a good fit for individuals who feel that traditional budgets are too restrictive. It also allows for a high degree of flexibility as any spending category can be substituted for another without a second thought. One month free cash flow may be allocated to dining while the next month it may be allocated to entertainment. Money can be allocated to a weekend getaway one month and to a new smartphone the next. The categories do not matter and do not need to be tracked as along as the total is within the target spending amount. The downside is that some people may have a tendency to overspend early in the month and then find that they do not have the cash flow to fund higher priority expenses later in the month. For example, going on a shopping spree early in the month and then not having enough money available to pay a utility bill at month-end. For this reason, this approach tends to work best for high-income households where there is plenty of money to fund needs and the focus is on limiting the amount spent on wants.

Financial Statement Approach:

There are three primary financial statements: an income and expense statement, a net worth statement, and a cash flow statement. An income and expense statement tracks all household income and expenses over a past period of time. A net worth statement lists household assets and liabilities as of a given date. A cash flow statement lists all cash inflows and outflows over a given period of time. The cash flow statement differs from the income and expense statement in that it captures savings and investment, which are not technically expenses, as well as principal payments on debt which also represent savings rather than expenses. (See appendix 1 for a description of how to create financial statements)

Once the financial statements are created, ratio analysis can be used to analyze them. There are three major categories of financial ratios: liquidity ratios, debt ratios, and savings ratios. Liquidity ratios can be used to measure an individual's ability to pay short-term debt obligations and meet emergency financial needs. Liquidity is a financial term that refers to the accessibility of cash reserves and investments. An asset that can be converted into cash quickly with little or no loss of value, such as a checking or savings account, is considered highly liquid. Liquidity ratios include the:

• Emergency fund ratio. This is the ratio of liquid assets to monthly expenses. A typical target for an emergency fund ratio is between 3:1 and 6:1. This means that an individual should have between 3 and 6 months of expenses in an accessible savings account. For example, if a household has a monthly budget of $5,000 the emergency fund should be between $15,000 ($5,000 x 3) and $30,000 ($5,000 x 6). If the emergency fund ratio is below 3:1 it may be difficult to deal with unexpected financial challenges. If the emergency fund ratio is above 6:1 then it could mean forgoing the higher return that the money could earn if it were invested.

• Current ratio. The current ratio shows the relationship between the liquid assets and short-term liabilities listed on a balance sheet. A target ratio of between 1:1 and 2:1 is desirable. For example, if a household has short-term financial obligations, such as monthly bills, a college tuition payment, and a credit card balance, of $50,000 there should be between $50,000 ($50,000 x 1) and $100,000 ($50,000 x 2) in liquid assets to meet this obligation. A ratio of less than 1:1 shows that the ability to meet short-term liabilities may be questionable. A ratio above 2:1 indicates that there may be too much money invested in short-term assets which could be invested for a longer period of time in an attempt to achieve higher returns.

Debt ratios are used to analyze a household's liabilities. Debt ratios gauge a household's ability to pay their debts based on their current financial situation. Debt ratios include the:

• Debt to assets ratio. This is a comparison of total debt to total assets. At a maximum the debt to assets ratio should be 1:1. For example, if the total of all household assets add up to $300,000 the total of the household debt should be $300,000 or less. A ratio greater than 1:1 indicates a negative net worth which means that the household owes more than it owns. If the debt to asset ratio is too high then an emphasis should be put on paying down debt. Over time the debt to assets ratio should decrease which indicates increasing wealth. This does not mean that borrowing is bad, instead it means that debt can increase as long as assets increase at a faster rate.

• Housing cost to monthly income ratio. This ratio is used to assess a borrower's ability to pay the expenses associated with home ownership. The expenses that make up housing costs are the principle and interest payments on all loans secured by the home plus the cost of property taxes, homeowner's insurance premiums, and association dues. Monthly income is defined as all monthly income from all sources on a before tax basis. Ideally housing costs should be no more than 28.5%

(ratio is 1:3.5) of monthly income. For example, a household with gross annual income of $8,000 per month should seek to spend $2,285 ($8,000 / 3.5) or less per month, on expenses directly linked to the home. If housing expenses exceed 28% of income it may impinge on the household's ability to fund other long-term financial goals.

• Housing cost and debt payments to monthly income ratio. This indicator adds the required payments on all other outstanding debts to housing costs. Required payments include payments on auto loans, credit cards, and student loans. The total of these payments and monthly housing costs should not exceed 36% (ratio is 1:2.8) of monthly income. Another way to consider this is that as long as the housing cost to income ratio is in-line with the previously mentioned target then other debt payments should not exceed 8% of the household's monthly income.

Saving ratios measure financial stability and progress towards financial goals. These ratios track the accumulation of assets and the periodic increase or decrease in their value. Saving ratios include the:

• Savings ratio. The savings ratio is the amount saved each month, including matching retirement contributions from an employer, compared to total pretax monthly income. The earlier that an individual begins saving the less that they may need to contribute each year to achieve their long-term financial goals. For this reason, the ideal savings ratio may be different based on the age an individual begins saving. An ideal savings ratio for someone who starts saving at a young age may be 1:7 (save $1 for every $7 earned) while the savings rate for someone who waits until they are older to start saving may increase to a ratio of 1:5 (save $1 for every $5 earned).

• Savings to desired annual retirement income ratio. This ratio is used to track progress toward retirement funding. After subtracting pension income, Social Security, and other retirement resources from the desired retirement income, a savings to income ratio of 25:1 is desirable. For example, if a household's desired retirement income is $60,000 per year and they expect to receive $25,000 from other sources they would need to replace $35,000 from savings. A savings to desired retirement income ratio of 25:1 would require saving of $875,000 ($35,000 x 25).

As with the other approaches to budgeting, financial statements and ratio analysis should be reviewed periodically. The ratio analysis will provide insight into the areas that need attention. If the savings ratio is too low, then an effort to increase savings should become a priority. If the debt to assets ratio is too high, an effort should be made to pay down debt. If more than one ratio is out of line with the target the ratios should be prioritized in following order, liquidity ratio tackled first, then debt ratios, and then savings ratios.

Each of the approaches to budgeting has its pros and cons. Therefore, it is impossible to say that one approach is better than the another. The most important thing is that a household finds the approach that best fits their needs and is most likely to result in financial success.

9

Fixed vs. Variable Expenses

One of the factors that investment analysts often review when analyzing a company is the ratio of fixed expenses and variable expense compared to the total expenses listed on a company's income statement. The fixed and variable expense ratios can be a way to assess the variability of a company's earnings when its revenue increases or decreases. Therefore, the relationship can be a way to assess both the potential risk and reward should the company perform well and increase revenues or hit a rough patch in which revenues fall.

Fixed and variable expenses may also have a large impact on household spending and saving patterns. The percentage of household expenses that are fixed versus variable may be an indication of how easily a household can adapt to an adverse economic environment.

Fixed costs are those that do not increase or decrease with revenue. They are obligations that are not tied directly to the income activities of the company such as the cost of maintaining company facilities and interest payments on long-term debt. For a household these expenses may be a rent or mortgage payment as well as debts that must be paid. These are the payments that must be paid regardless of changes in income.

Variable costs are those that increase or decrease with revenue. For a company these may include the compensation paid to sales staff, the costs of goods sold, and interest paid on trade credit. For example, when a company's sales increase it is likely to pay more in sales commissions to its sales staff. On the other hand, when sales decline the amount paid in sales commissions is likely to decline as well. For a household these expenses may include commuting costs, the cost of child care so both parents can work, or the cost of eating out due to time constraints created by a busy work schedule. If an individual is not working, or working reduced hours, these expenses may decline providing some financial flexibility that will allow the household to adapt to the change in income.

The variable expense ratio is the variable expenses divided by total expenses while the fixed expense ratio is the fixed expenses divided by total expenses. A company or household with a high fixed expense ratio and a low variable expense ratio generally is higher risk than a company with more balance ratios. As revenue increases a company or households fixed costs generally remain the same. The variable expenses increase but may only represent a small percentage of the increased revenue or income. Therefore, a large portion of the additional revenue will flow to the bottom line creating a larger percentage increase in earnings for a company and saving for a household.

On the other hand, if a company's revenue or a household's income declines the fixed expenses will remain the same. Variable expenses may decrease as well but only by a small amount. So, the decline in revenue will largely fall to the bottom line resulting in a larger percentage decrease in earnings for a company or savings for a household.

On the other hand, a company or household with low fixed costs and high variable costs will experience lower earnings or savings volatility. When revenues or income increases the high variable costs will offset a large portion of the increase so that earnings or savings increase by a small percentage. Meanwhile, when revenue or income declines the reduction in variable costs will offset a large percentage of the decrease.

In other words, a high level of fixed costs and low level of variable costs leads to increased risk that a household will not be able to meet its financial obligations during bad financial times. Meanwhile, a low level of fixed costs and a high level of variable costs gives a household more flexibility to adapt to periods of variable income.

For a household, fixed costs include debt payments such as mortgage payments, auto loan payments, and student loan payments. In addition, there are expenses that are a nondiscretionary part of a household's standard of living including property taxes, insurance premiums, and many day-to-day living expenses. Variable expenses include income taxes as well as discretionary expenses such as eating out, vacations, and a new big screen television. Savings can also be a way to protect a household from income variability because it can be increased or decreased without forcing a change in the household's overall lifestyle.

If a household has a high fixed expense ratio and a low variable expense ratio a decrease in income can make it very difficult to pay the fixed expenses as there will be relatively few variable expenses that can be reduced.

This may lead to missed debt payments as well as unpaid property taxes or insurance premiums and a potentially painful reduction in the household's standard of living. Ideally, a household should strive to be in a position to be able to pay their fixed expenses at all times.

A household that maintains a low fixed expense ratio and a high variable expense ratio will be able to withstand financial hardship much better than one with a high fixed costs ratio. When household income decreases due to job loss, an economic recession that leads to lower wages, or a decrease in investment values that reduce investment income, the variable expenses can be reduced. For example, income taxes will typically decline with income, the amount saved can be reduced, and vacations or large purchases can be postponed. This will reduce the impact that the loss of income will have on the household's bottom line and make it more likely that they will be able to pay their fixed costs.

Meanwhile, if a household has a low fixed costs ratio an increase in income will give them the flexibility to determine how to allocate their excess financial resources. The additional income can be saved to build up an emergency reserve or to fund longer-term financial goals. In addition, the money can be used to fund one-off expenses such as a vacation or a large expenditure such as a new car or home improvements. As long as the expenses funded do not represent an ongoing increase in the household standard of living those expenses will remain variable expenses which may be reduced in the future if needed.

Fixed costs should only be incurred when there is a high level of confidence that they can be maintained through good times and bad. If it is unclear that income will be available over the long-term to support a fixed expense it is better to save to make the purchase or accumulate a nest egg that can fund the higher standard of living before making any long-term commits.

10

Household Inflation Rate

istorically the rate of inflation (the pace at which prices rise over time) has been a big concern for American households. This is especially true for retirees who are on a fixed income as inflation can quickly erode the purchasing power of their limited financial resources. However, in recent years workers have also become more and more focused on inflation risk as wages have failed to keep pace with the increase in the general level of prices. Yet the impact that inflation is likely to have on an individual household's spending may vary greatly based on the pattern of household spending. This can lead to each household having a unique inflation rate that may differ from the inflation rate published in national and regional statistics.

The primary determinant of the difference between a household's inflation rate and the inflation statistics that are published each month by the Bureau of Labor Statistics (BLS) is the difference between the household's spending patterns and the weights that are given to the different spending categories in the national and regional statistics. For example, the national statistics assume that the average household's spending is allocated 13.6% to food, 7.5% to energy, 18.7% to goods, 33.9% to shelter, 6.7% to medical services, 6.0%

to transportation, and 13.6% to other services. The inflation rate for each of these categories may be higher or lower than the average at different times. Therefore, to the extent that a household spends a greater or lesser amount in each category the household's inflation rate may differ from the average.

A household can manage its inflation rate by changing its spending patterns. For example, food and energy prices are notoriously volatile. So, to the extent that a household can limit its spending in these categories it may be able to reduce its inflation risk. One way to do this is to emphasize energy efficiency. Buying an energy efficient vehicle can reduce the amount of spending on gasoline which is 3.5% of the average household's spending. Choosing a vehicle that is relatively safe and dependable can also make a difference as a large portion of transportation services expenses are allocated to vehicle maintenance and insurance expenses. Therefore, a vehicle that is relatively inexpensive to maintain and insure can reduce the exposure to the variability of prices in the transportation services category. In addition, household energy costs represent another 3.6% of spending on average. Purchasing an energy efficient home or making energy efficient upgrades can limit the exposure to the volatility of energy prices potentially reducing the household inflation rate in the process.

Food is another volatile category which represents 7.8% of average household spending. However, the bulk of this category is allocated to "food away from home" as opposed to "food at home." Therefore, a household has a lot of flexibility in reducing their food expenses by choosing where to eat based on the cost effectiveness. It is also possible to manage the personal inflation rate by weighing substitutes. For example, when beef prices are high chicken can be substituted in its place. In this way a little monitoring and planning can reduce the inflation risk from high food prices.

Another factor is the definitions that are used for some of the spending categories. For example, "owner's equivalent rent of residences" represents 24.7% of the average household's spending. This is an estimate of the amount that an owner of a home would have to pay, or would receive, if they were to rent their home. While this may be a relatively accurate measure of the rental value of a home it really has no bearing on the actual inflation rate for a household that owns a home. In fact, if the home was purchased with a fixed rate mortgage the mortgage payment will remain the same whether the rental value of the home increases or decreases over time. Those who own their home outright will not have rent or mortgage related expenses which can cause their inflation rate to deviate greatly from the average. For example, during the housing bust in the late-2000s the value and rental rates for homes declined leading to deflation (prices falling) rather than inflation. However, a household that owned their home with a fixed mortgage or owned the home outright did not experience a decrease in housing related expenses. Therefore, the household's inflation rate was likely positive even while the nation as a whole was experiencing deflation. Conversely, when the housing market recovered, housing prices and rents climbed sharply leading to an increase in owner equivalent rents which put some upward pressure on inflation. However, the increase in these expenses did not affect some households leading to very different inflation rates depending on the household's circumstances.

Finally, the methodology used to determine the nation's inflation rate can cause the published inflation rates to deviate from the experience of many households. One of the important factors is that the national inflation statistics do not take into account the impact of improved quality. So goods that become obsolete very quickly, such as technology, are considered deflationary as a new state-of-the-art computer, cell phone, or television may be expensive when first released but will likely sell for much less when the new generation is released. Since the new generation is considered higher quality due to upgrades in technology the price increase from one generation to another is not captured. Instead it is assumed that the cost of technology decreases over time even though this is not the experience of the average household.

This means a household of early adopters who want to own the newest and best technology may have a much higher inflation rate than those who are willing to wait for prices to decline before purchasing. In addition, allowing several generations of new products to come out before upgrading can space out the costs incurred making it a source of inflationary pressure every three to five years instead of a year-to-year issue.

Households that take these factors into consideration may be able to manage their inflation rate more effectively than those that do not understand the impact that their spending patterns may have on the prices that they pay. In addition, estimating a household's inflation rate can be useful when attempting to mitigate inflation risk by matching the inflation risk associated with the different forms of household income to the household inflation risk.

For example, a retiree with a large percentage of their income coming from a pension may have a high level of inflation risk. Many pension benefits do not increase with inflation and those that do often have a cap as to how much the benefit will increase in a given year. Therefore, a period of high inflation can quickly reduce the purchasing power of a pension. In this case the retiree may choose to not pay off their mortgage in retirement and instead invest the money in assets that are expected to increase with inflation. A fixed rate mortgage payment, which will not increase in cost with the rate of inflation, can be used to average down the retiree's personal inflation rate. Assume that a fixed rate mortgage payment represents 20% of a retiree's expenses with their other expenses subject to inflation risk. If the general level of prices increases 5% the retiree would only experience a 4% increase in household expenses because only 80% of their expenses would increase by 5% (5% x 80% = 4%) while 20% of their expenses (the fixed rate mortgage payment) would not increase. Therefore, maintaining a mortgage could reduce the retiree's personal inflation rate by a full percentage point which may reduce the risk of household expenses increasing at a much faster pace than their pension income.

On the other hand, a household that has income that is likely to be correlated with inflation such as rental income, stock dividends, or government benefits that are indexed to inflation may reduce their risk by attempting to match the household inflation rate to the national rate of inflation. This can be done by paying off debts that have a fixed payment and attempting to match household spending patterns to the spending categories used in the national inflation calculations. That way if the nation goes through a period of deflation, so that household income stagnates or declines, the household is likely to experience an offsetting decrease in expenses.

Understanding inflation is an important part of managing household inflation risk. This includes knowing how inflation is calculated, what actions can be taken to reduce a household's inflation risk, and estimating a household's inflation rate. Inflation risk can be mitigated by matching the estimated Cost Of Living Adjustment (COLA) for household income with the household's inflation rate. This way the risk of a substantial increase or decrease in inflation may be managed and mitigated.

11

What is the Real Cost?

Often Americans understand financial concepts such as debt financing, inflation, and taxes but they do not know how to apply them when making financial decisions. In other words, people can explain what the concepts mean but they fail to apply them to their own situation in order to make more informed financial choices. This can lead to poor spending decisions as consumers often do not consider the full cost of the purchases that they make.

For example, when making a purchase it may be important to account for sales taxes. With many state and local governments increasing their sales tax rates in order to fund local services and underfunded pension obligations, sales taxes are becoming a larger and larger portion of the total cost of making a purchase. Factoring in sales taxes is especially important when considering large purchases like a vehicle as the sales tax can add thousands of dollars to the overall purchase price.

Personal property taxes must also be taken into account when making large purchases. The cost of paying real estate taxes on a home can add up to a substantial sum over a long holding period.

Registration costs for a vehicle can also add up and contribute to the total cost of ownership. These taxes are often based on the purchase price of the home or vehicle so that the total cost of ownership typically increases in-line with the purchase price.

Of course, income and employment taxes must also be taken into consideration. An individual who is in a high income tax bracket may need to generate income well in excess of the list price to net the money needed to make a purchase. In many cases the amount of earnings required to fund a purchase may be one and a half times the purchase price. For example, an individual facing a 24% federal income tax bracket, a 7% state income tax bracket, and a sales tax rate of 6% will need to earn an additional $152 in order to fund a purchase of $100. Therefore, a vehicle that costs an additional $10,000 over a less costly option will require an additional $15,200 of earnings to fund. This does not mean that the purchase should be avoided but it should be weighed against the actual cost in terms of the gross income that must be committed when the purchasing decision is made.

The after-tax cost does not include any additional financing costs. A purchase that is financed can include substantial interest costs. For example, payments on a 30-year mortgage can add an amount equal to the amount borrowed to the real purchase price as half of the total payments will be allocated to interest. A five-year auto loan with a low interest rate can add 15% to the total cost of the vehicle. It is important to factor in these costs before making a purchase decision or deciding how much of a down payment to make on a home or vehicle. It is also important to note that home mortgage and auto loan interest rates are relatively modest compared to credit card or personal loan interest rates. Therefore, consumer purchases that are made on credit and not paid off within a short time period can cost far more than even the after-tax cost when interest costs are factored in.

After a purchase is made, maintenance and upkeep expenses continue to add to the total cost of the purchase. For a vehicle this is called the total cost of ownership. It includes the cost of fuel, anticipated maintenance costs, insurance, and the decrease in the value of the car each year. This information can be found online for different vehicle makes and models. In general, vehicles that are more fuel efficient and dependable have a lower cost of ownership. For personal vehicles these costs are paid on an after-tax basis so the total cost including taxes should be incorporated into the calculation as well. Unfortunately, there are no total costs of ownership statistics for homes. However, like vehicles, homes age and things need to be replaced. In addition, a home must be insured and the property taxes must be paid. This can make the total cost of home ownership well in excess of the monthly mortgage payment.

When all of the different costs are added to the costs of a purchase the real financial cost emerges. As the expenses compound, even a substantial household income can be whittled away very quickly. Therefore, it is important to take all of these costs into account when choosing how to best allocate limited resources. Impulse purchases can not only lead to paying more than one needs to for an item, it can also lead to ongoing costs in the form of interest payments, taxes, and the ongoing cost of ownership. When the real cost of making a purchase is taken into account it may cause a consumer to pause to consider whether the purchase is a priority or if the money should be spent more wisely.

12

Phantom Debt

I t is quite common to read about the dangers of over borrowing. Naturally, depending on future income to pay for past purchases is always somewhat risky as the future is inherently uncertain and therefore the expected income may not materialize. In addition, borrowing often comes with additional costs in the form of interest expenses, loan fees, etc. which may increase the total cost of a purchase. However, many people engage in a form of phantom borrowing which they may not even be aware of but can be just as dangerous as borrowing using conventional loans.

Any time an individual commits future money to pay an expense or other financial obligation they are in essence borrowing on the future. They are committing future cash flows to pay for an expense or obligation that was incurred but not yet due. In some cases, this may come with some additional costs while in others there may be no downside to delaying the payment unless it becomes habitual. Habitual phantom borrowing can cause an individual to fall into a financial hole that can be very hard to dig out of without substantial costs.

Perhaps one of the most common forms of phantom borrowing is income taxes. The United States has a pay-as-you-go tax system. This means that income tax is due when money is earned. For employees the tax is typically paid through payroll tax withholding that comes directly out of their paycheck. Sometimes they may pay in a bit too much or a bit too little so they settle-up with the IRS after the end of the year and either pay the amount owed or receive a refund if they paid in too much during the year. People who are self-employed or do not receive their income through a method that allows for tax withholding typically make quarterly estimated tax payments to pay the IRS the amount they estimate that they owe for the quarter. If the estimates are accurate they should owe a small amount or receive a small refund when they file their taxes for the year.

The problem comes when an individual falls behind on their tax payments. For example, they may not have enough withheld from their paycheck or may not pay a sufficient amount in estimated payments. This can put them in the difficult situation of depending on their earnings between the end of the year and the tax filing deadline in April to accumulate a sufficient amount to cover their tax bill for the prior year. In essence they have borrowed from their tax account and then must scramble to come up with the money to pay the bill when it comes due. This borrowing may accrue interest in the form of an underpayment penalty assessed by the IRS. There is also the risk that the individual is not able to gather the money to cover their tax bill by the filing deadline in which case they will need to set up a payment plan with the IRS which will be subject to additional fees and interest turning their phantom borrowing into a more formal debt obligation.

In some cases a self-employed individual may be able to come up with the money to pay their tax bill by the filing deadline but the amount owed is based on the assumption that a sizable tax-deductible retirement plan contribution will be made for the previous year. For some such retirement plans the due date for the contribution is the tax extension deadline in October. So they must work from January to April to cover their tax bill and then work from April to October to accumulate the money to make their retirement plan contribution. In other words, it takes ten months to settle the tax and retirement obligations for the prior year. This is akin to having borrowed ten months of savings from the previous year. Even if there is no interest charged on the debt the individual risks falling into a perpetual trap of using future cash flows to pay for past obligations.

Often the problem of phantom borrowing comes to light when there is a change in the individual's circumstances. For example, if an individual's business hits a rough patch they may not be able to come up with the money to pay off the tax obligation on money earned in a prior year. In addition, if they cannot accumulate the money to contribute to their retirement plan they may owe even more in taxes which they may not have the money to pay.

Another challenge is when an individual seeks to retire. Since they are depending on future earnings to settle their tax and retirement obligations from past years they cannot stop working and earning or they will be short the cash flow needed to make those payments. Therefore, they may be stuck working and saving in an attempt to earn enough to cover the tax on their current earnings and the amount that is owed on past earnings. If an individual's tax rate is high enough it may be nearly impossible to play catch-up and settle their phantom debts making it impossible to retire.

Another form of phantom borrowing comes in the form of the depreciation of personal use assets. For example, as a vehicle ages and accumulates more miles its value is being used up and eventually it will need to be replaced. If the vehicle was purchased for $40,000 and is expected to last for 8 years its use value is depreciating by $5,000 per year on average. Therefore, if an individual does not save at least $5,000 per year to use toward a replacement vehicle they are actually engaging in phantom borrowing as they are counting on future cash flows to replace the useful life of the vehicle that they have used up in the past. If not corrected they will get to the end of the useful life of the vehicle and will likely have to borrow to purchase a new one at which point the phantom debt will be converted into an actual debt in the form of a car loan.

This same principle applies to homeownership. It is fairly common for an individual pay off their home mortgage only to turn around and borrow on their home equity to install a new roof or remodel their kitchen. This occurs because while they targeted their financial resources at paying off their actual debt they accumulated a phantom debt in the form of wear and tear on the home. After the actual debt is paid off they then must convert their phantom debt into an actual debt to bring the property back to its original state.

Finally, any future financial obligation that has not yet been paid but is not a part of a formal debt obligation can be considered a phantom debt. If an individual has committed to a nonrefundable vacation and is making payments it could be considered a phantom debt. An alimony or child support obligation is a phantom debt. Even a commitment to fund a child's future education expenses may be considered a phantom debt. These obligations may not be documented in a formal debt agreement but to the extent that future cash flows must be used to pay for a commitment or obligation that was made in the past a debt has been incurred and should be accounted for.

A complete look at an individual's financial circumstances should include these phantom debts. They may not show up on an individual's net worth statement or be included in their budget but they can have a real impact on their overall financial picture. Phantom debts will eventually need to be paid. If not addressed they may be converted into actual debt which can have a negative impact on an otherwise solid financial plan.

13

The Next Best Alternative Standard

I t is no secret that Americans have not done a very good job of saving for the future. Every year there are multiple surveys reporting that a large percentage of American households do not have sufficient financial reserves to cover a surprise expense of $1,000 or more. Instead of saving a large portion of their income American households are more likely to borrow on their expected future income so that they are constantly digging out of a pit of debt, trying to just get back to even, never mind getting ahead. This leads to low levels of financial security in which even a small financial emergency can be a major blow to many households.

One problem is that the largest determinants of an individual's spending are their current income and their expectations for future income. In other words, individuals tend to spend what they make. The exception is when an individual expects their income to increase in the future in which case they spend more than they make by borrowing. So when a financial emergency occurs or the expectation for future income proves to be overly optimistic it can create a difficult financial situation.

One reason for the poor state of many households' finances is a lack of income to maintain a minimum standard of living. There are many households that report income near or below the poverty line which leaves little money to be saved for financial emergencies and may force them to borrow to purchase basic necessities. However, there are also many households with more than sufficient income to cover their basic household needs that still find themselves over extended financially. These households may benefit from taking a different mindset when it comes to spending and saving decisions.

One general rule that can be used to avoid financial distress is for a household to live a standard of living based on their next best alternative. The next best alternative is the most attractive option should an individual's current situation not work out. For example, if an individual were to lose their current job how much do they believe they could earn if they were forced to start over with a new employer given their current level of education and experience? If an individual's income is variable, which is the case for many who are self-employed or work in sales, the next best alternative may be the amount they would expect to be able to earn if their income decreased due to an economic recession or cyclical industry factors. For someone who is retired the next best alternative may be the amount they can reasonably take from retirement accounts during a poor market environment while still meeting their financial needs. It basically accounts for the possibility of negative financial events and pegs spending targets to the amount of income that is likely to be available even during a period of financial difficulty.

Spending according to the next best alternative has two benefits. The first is that if a household determines its spending targets based on its next best alternative it is likely to save a reasonable portion of its income when things work out as planned. This will allow the household to build an emergency fund, pay down debts, and plan for longer-term financial goals. The second benefit is that should a negative financial event occur in which the household is forced to implement its next best alternative the financial adjustments that are needed will likely be fairly mild. This will increase the likelihood that the household will not be forced to drastically reduce its standard of living to survive a financial emergency or difficult period for the economy which may impact the labor markets and financial markets.

Another benefit of spending according to the next best alternative is that it can help an individual avoid being relegated to accepting an even worse outcome. Often when an individual is exposed to financial stress and does not have sufficient financial flexibility or reserves they must take whatever opportunities are available rather than being able to hold out for a better option. Meanwhile, those that do have some financial stability may be able to get by for a time allowing them to wait for better opportunities to materialize. For example, if an individual with little financial flexibility loses their job they may be forced to take the first offer that comes available, even if it comes with greatly reduced compensation, to survive financially. However, an individual with financial flexibility and reserves can take some time to review their options and even reject offers below a minimum level of compensation which may increase the likelihood that they will find employment that is in-line with their next best alternative. A retiree with little financial flexibility that is faced with sharp declines in the financial markets may be forced to continue to take distributions from their investments despite the depressed values. This may force them to lock in losses on their accounts so that the future income that their investments can support is permanently reduced. Meanwhile, a retiree that has the flexibility to reduce their distributions until their account balances recover may not suffer the same negative long-term impact from the market downturn.

Ideally, a household's next best alternative will increase over time allowing for an increase in spending and standard of living. Yet spending will consistently be below the amount household income could support unless it is a period of financial strain. This will maintain a gap between income and spending which can be saved for the future and create the financial flexibility the household may need to avoid major setbacks and long-term financial distress.

14

Cycles

C ycles are a part of the natural world. Each day is a cycle in which the sun rises and then sets only to repeat the process the next day. Every year is a cycle as the seasons come and go in a pattern that repeats year after year. There are also the cycles that influence the tides, ocean currents, global wind patterns, animal populations and so on. These cycles along with many others are a natural part of the human experience as we navigate our way through an ever-changing world. Cycles are also a part of the financial world. Therefore, it is important to understand the financial cycles and the impact they may have on a financial plan.

In the financial world cycles can be classified into four categories: Seasonal cycles, trend cycles, super cycles, and life cycles. Seasonal cycles are typically the shortest of the four cycles as they tend to repeat each year, although the magnitude of the changes often vary from year to year. For example, the price of some commodities, such as natural gas and heating oil, change based on the weather. During the winter months increased demand for heating often drives the prices of these commodities up and then they decline as the weather gets warmer. Gasoline prices often follow a counter cycle to natural gas and heating oil as gasoline prices tend to increase in the summer months when people drive more and then decline during the fall. Consumer spending also follows seasonal patterns as spending often surges during the holiday season in November and December as well as during other periods such as the back-to-school season. In addition, economic data may follow seasonal cycles. Construction activity and employment tend to be higher when the weather is warm and then decline when cold weather makes it more challenging to build. In fact, economists often report seasonally adjusted economic data which is an attempt to remove the impact that seasonal cycles have on the economic data. However, it is important to note that these seasonal adjustments are not perfect as factors such as the weather do not follow perfect patterns from year to year. An unusually warm winter, a natural disaster, or high unemployment during a normally high consumer spending period among other factors can impact the seasonal cycles and distort the data.

Seasonal cycles are generally anticipated by the financial markets so that the seasonal changes in prices are unlikely to yield any consistent return opportunities. However, seasonal factors can be an important consideration when it comes to budgeting. It is important to account for the seasonal increases in home energy bills, holiday spending, and gasoline prices just to name a few of spending categories that may exhibit a high degree of variability. In addition, those who work in industries that are subject to seasonal cycles need to prepare for periods when their income may decline by saving when their income is high. This way they will be prepared for periods of lower income and/or periods of elevated expenses.

Unlike seasonal cycles, trend cycles often last much longer than one year and the length of the cycles often vary. For example, the business cycle, which is the boom and bust cycle of the economy, has an average duration of five years with some cycles as short as 18 months and some as long as 10 years. Trend cycles may have a long-term positive trend that overlays the shorter-term cyclical ups and downs. An example is the major stock market indices which periodically have short periods where returns are well above the long-term average and then short periods of losses, yet the long-term trend is positive. This means that each cyclical high is often above the previous high and the corresponding cyclical low is generally above the low from the previous cycle.

There are also negative trend cycles in which the long-term trend is downward despite shorter-term ups and downs. For example, US interest rates have exhibited an overall negative trend since 1980. Generally, interest rates have been correlated with the business cycle so they have increased when the economy is growing and decreased when the economy is contracting but the overall longer-term trend has been downward.

Of course, there are periods when a positive trend cycle may transition into a negative trend cycle and vice versa. Therefore, it is important not to put too much faith in a cycle no matter how long the positive or negative trend has persisted. Often when a trend cycle is viewed as a given it will reverse catching a large number of people unprepared.

Trend cycles are very important when it comes to financial planning. Specifically, the business cycle and the other cycles that are correlated with the business cycle should be monitored closely. The phase of the business cycle (growth, contraction, recession, and recovery) should be taken into account when making financial decisions. For example, individuals should be careful when taking on long-term debt obligations during the late growth phase of the business cycle. Often individuals feel most confident about their financial situation following a long period of economic recovery and then growth. However, if the economy is in the late growth stage the next stage will likely be contraction where the income or investments that were expected to be used to pay back the debt may decline. This is especially true when purchasing an asset like real estate which often increases in value when the economy and household incomes are increasing and decreases in value or stagnates when the business cycle is in the contraction or recession phase.

The stock market and interest rate trend cycles are correlated with the business cycle. Therefore, investment decisions should take these cycles into consideration. When the business cycle contracts the stock market often declines and interest rates fall causing bond values to increase. Increasing investment risk by selling bonds and buying stocks during the growth phase can lead to short-term gains but greater losses when the business cycle enters the contraction and then recession phase. Similarly, selling stocks to purchase bonds during the recession phase can be damaging to a financial plan as the returns may be subpar when the business cycle transitions to the recovery and then growth phase.

While miscalculating a trend cycle can be damaging to a financial plan, being on the wrong side of a super cycle can lead to financial disaster. Super cycles come from supply and demand mismatches in areas of the economy where supply cannot respond quickly to changes in demand. In these cases, there is often a lag between changes in demand and an increase or decrease in supply but when supply does adjust it often over does it as many suppliers all change their behavior in response to the change in demand and prices. This can lead to big price increases when demand is growing and supply is unable to keep up due to the large investment of time and money that may be required to increase supply. This is followed by big decreases in prices when demand slows and suppliers continue to increase supply in an attempt to recover the money they invested in order to increase their capacity to supply the market. The suppliers that are able to navigate the downturn are then slow to increase supply when demand later recovers allowing the cycle to start again. Super cycles tend to be very long-term, often lasting decades, and the price changes are often much greater than can be imagined beforehand.

Super cycles are often associated with manias or bubbles. For example, in the mid-2000s low interest rates and increased demand for houses pushed prices upward. The positive price trend attracted first-time homebuyers and investors to the market which further increased demand. However, houses cannot be built very quickly as it can take years for builders to secure the land, get permits to build, install needed infrastructure, and finally start building a home. Therefore, supply was slow to respond to the increase in demand allowing prices to increase at above average rates for several years. With prices continuously climbing many builders rushed to get to the building phase and planned larger and larger developments. All were racing to be first to market and capture as much market share as possible. When this supply finally came to market it soon overwhelmed demand. At the market peak new household formation was just 1.5 million per year while 2.2 million new homes were being built. There were more homes than there were people to live in them. Eventually, demand declined and prices fell but developers continued building new houses. After all, they had borrowed to acquire the land, pay for permits, and install necessary infrastructure so they had debt payments to make. As long as the home could sell for more than the additional investment required to complete construction the builder would finish it in order to secure the money to pay debts. The continued increase in supply in the face or waning demand drove prices down to the point where even a project that was mostly built-out was not economical to complete. In some cases, prices were less than half the total cost to build the home.

Supply growth then stalled while demand slowly recovered as some buyers were lured into the market by the bargain prices. This caused the price trend to reverse attracting still more buyers and demand slowly recovered. However, builders were cautious in responding to the increase in demand following their large losses during the housing bust. Soon there was a housing supply shortage in many markets causing prices and rents to increase sharply. During the super cycle prices more than doubled, then fell by more than half, only to once again more than double to reach new highs.

Similar super cycles have been observed in technology stocks, oil, and cryptocurrencies. Limited supply leads to an increase in prices which stokes further demand causing prices to surge. Eventually supply surges in response to the high prices whether in the form of poorly conceived technology IPOs, fracking oil and gas wells, or cryptocurrency ICOs (Initial Coin Offerings). As supply overcomes demand prices crash. Falling prey to one of these manias or bubbles can create a financial setback so great that it could take decades to recover.

Finally, life cycles are an important part of the natural and financial world. In the natural world the life cycle involves life and death. This also applies to the financial world as financial strategies change as people age making it important to plan based on life cycle considerations. For example, when it comes to investing the stage of an individual's life cycle can determine the investment risk that they should take. Someone who is early in their life cycle may be able to take more risk due to their earning power and long time horizon. Meanwhile someone who is late in their life cycle may need to take less risk due to the shorter time horizon and possible need to access the money to pay expenses. In addition, insurance needs may be affected by the stage of an individual's life cycle (see Risk Management with Limited Resources). Not to mention the decisions of when to retire, when to divest of a privately held business, when to create an estate plan and how it should be structured, etc. The life cycle plays an important role in all of these decisions.

However, in the financial world the life cycle is not limited to an individual's mortality. Assets have life cycles as well. For example, a vehicle will only last so long before the end of its life cycle. Therefore, vehicles may need to be replaced every so many years which should be factored into an individual's budget. Real estate also has a life cycle in which replacement costs begin to add up. For example, the cost of new appliances, replacing a deck or roof, or remodeling a kitchen may all be a function of the life cycle of the property. It is easy to ignore these costs on a day-to-day basis but in the longer-term they can be substantial and should be anticipated so that there is sufficient savings or home equity to make the improvements.

Companies have life cycles as well. Companies start in the start-up stage in which investor capital is raised to fund the venture and the market for the company's goods or services is tested. If investors are willing to fund the venture and the market is viable the company may transition into the growth stage in which sales increase at a fast pace but profit is still fairly low. Eventually sales reach a level where the growth rate naturally slows but profitability increases at which point the company is in the mature stage. Finally, if the company is unable to keep up with changes in its market or makes poor management choices the company may enter the decline stage where sales fall and profitability suffers. If the decline stage is not reversed it can eventually lead to the company being acquired or shutdown.

The company life cycle is important for investors who purchase stocks (own shares in companies) or corporate bonds (making loans to companies). A company that is early in its life cycle may be too risky as there is a high probability that the endeavor will fail to attract sufficient investment or customers for the products or services offered. In this case, the company may fail to reach the growth or mature stage where investors may profit. In addition, a company that is in the decline stage is similarly dangerous to invest in as what may seem like a temporary challenge may prove to be the companies undoing causing it to fail.

Being aware of the many types of financial cycles is an important aspect of financial planning. All financial planning decisions should be made with the cyclical nature of the economy and financial markets in mind. The good times do not last forever and the bad times are often temporary. The risks and rewards of the cyclical nature of the world should be balanced in order to participate in the rewards while managing and mitigating the risks.

15

The Debt Cycle

T he boom and bust nature of the economy is often a mystery. Predictably after every economic downturn there is the question: How did this happen and what can we do to prevent it from happening again? Typically, a narrative eventually emerges which people accept, but do not fully understand, leaving a feeling of increased uncertainty and the belief that there is a randomness to the forces that affect the economy and by extension household finances.

Every economic cycle has its own unique characteristics that either cause the business cycle to transition from the growth phase to the contraction phase or that cause the depth of the economic contraction to be larger or smaller than average. A factor that is present in nearly every recession but often goes overlooked is the debt cycle which is an important part of why economies expand and then contract in a repeating pattern.

Consumer spending accounts for approximately two-thirds of US economic output. Therefore, when consumer spending is growing at a healthy pace the economy is likely to follow suit. On the other hand, when consumer spending is declining the economy will likely shrink leading to a recession. Consumer spending can be funded from three sources: Income, savings, or debt.

Naturally the most common way to fund consumer spending is to fund it from current income. If everyone only spends what they earn then money will be passed throughout the economy and the rate of economic growth and the rate of consumer spending will be in-line with each other. Therefore, the rate of economic growth will be constrained to the rate of income growth, but recessions would also likely be less common.

When consumer spending is funded with savings, the rate of economic growth can exceed the rate of income growth as consumer spending will no longer be constrained by income growth. However, if consumers are drawing on their savings to fund current spending their savings will eventually be depleted and the rate of economic growth will slow to the pace of income growth. The withdrawal of savings-fueled spending can lead to a recession if the excess spending declines too quickly.

Consumer spending that is supported by debt can similarly cause the rate of economic growth to exceed the pace of income growth. When consumers borrow, they are committing future income to make purchases in the current period. However, this also cannot last as debt will eventually get so large that too much future income becomes committed to debt payments. This will naturally cause the pace of consumer spending to slow as income is used to pay debts rather than make new purchases and the economy will slip into recession.

The debt cycles mirrors the economic cycle. When the economy is in the growth phase consumers often feel confident about the stability of their future income. This may encourage them to spend down their savings as they feel they have a reduced need for a financial safety net. In addition, consumers may be more likely to take on debt as they expect to have the income needed in the future to make the debt payments but prefer to make the purchases today rather than wait until they have saved the money needed to make the purchase.

When the savings available for spending is depleted and the amount of debt that can be supported by future income reaches a logical limit the cycle turns. The pace of consumer spending naturally slows and may eventually decline. When consumer spending declines the level of household income also declines as the demand for the goods and services that workers provide in exchange for compensation falls. This can lead to a downturn in the economy as the level of economic output (the value of goods and services produced) declines. At this point consumers may no longer feel very confident about the stability of their future income causing them to cut back on spending to pay down debts or increase savings in order to be in a stronger financial position should their income decline in the future. A household does not even need to be directly affected by the contraction in consumer spending to change their behavior. If consumers see others around them struggling financially they will likely respond by taking action to improve their own finances in order to avoid the same fate.

Eventually debt is repaid or discharged in bankruptcy and short-term savings are rebuilt. Consumers start to feel more optimistic about their financial situation and spending starts to increase again. At this stage the cycle starts all over as consumers once again begin to spend down their savings and take on debt due to a feeling of increased financial stability.

So what can individual households do to protect themselves from the dangers of the debt cycle? The first step is to engage in contrarian thinking. Or as the legendary investor Warren Buffett put it: "The less prudence with which others conduct their affairs, the greater prudence with which we should conduct our own affairs." When other consumers are confidently spending down savings or taking on debt to fund increased spending it may be a good time to increase short-term savings and pay down debts in anticipation of a potential decrease in income in the future. Then when consumer spending slows due to the depleted savings and high debts of others it may be a good time to use short-term savings to make purchases. This is especially true when it comes to high cost purchases such as a home or car. When the economy is in recession and consumer spending is declining there are often opportunities to purchase these items at prices much lower than they sell for during the boom periods when consumers are competing to make purchases and are bidding up prices.

Ironically, if enough households engaged in this strategy many recessions would be avoided or at least would be much milder than they have been historically. Financial prudence at the individual level could lead to increased stability and consistent growth for the economic system as a whole. In other words, if enough people act to reduce the economic risk at their household level it will reduce the risk at the national level by making it less likely that a painful recession will occur. Unfortunately, not enough people think this way. When conservative households manage their risk by prudently saving and using debt responsibly it creates an incentive for others to take on more risk in order to take advantage of the perceived stability. This added risk eventually spreads to a tipping point in which too many households have increased their financial risk and the debt cycle turns.

The debt cycle can be monitored by tracking the level of household debt, the household debt service ratio, the pace of consumer spending compared to household income, and interest rates. When household debt reaches a high level it is prudent to start to worry about a downturn in consumer spending and the eventual reversal of the debt cycle. If the level of household debt starts to decline this may be a sign that households are using income to pay down debt rather than spend. A decrease in spending could lead to an recession. However, at that point it may be too late for individual households to change their behavior in time to accumulate the short-term savings needed to make it through the recession. Therefore, it is important to start planning for a downturn in the economy before household debt peaks.

The household debt service ratio is the percentage of household income that is used to fund debt payments. When the household debt service ratio is increasing it is a sign that a larger percentage of household income is committed to paying for past purchases which may reduce their ability to keep spending at the same pace in the future. Therefore, unless household income increases, and the pace of debt accumulation slows, it may begin to weigh on consumer spending and economic growth.

When the pace of consumer spending outpaces the increase in household income it is a sign that consumer spending is being fueled by a reduction in short-term savings or an increase in household debt. This can persist for many years but eventually household income is the primary driver of consumer spending. Therefore, a large deviation between the two data points over a prolonged time period should be a concern.

Interest rates can also have an impact on the debt cycle. When interest rates are low consumers do not have to commit as much of their future income to make current purchases. However, when interest rates are increasing it may deter consumers from borrowing to fund current spending and the cost of existing debt may increase reducing the amount available to spend. Therefore, the level of interest rates should be monitored closely.

Monitoring the economic data that changes with the phases of the debt cycle can be a valuable consideration when making household spending decisions. It is important for households to take the overall environment into account rather than just focusing on their individual circumstances. Taking such an approach may allow individual households to avoid some of the negative effects from an economic recession so that they can better stay on track to achieve their financial goals.

16

The Asymmetry of Wealth Creation

I nvestment planning typically focuses on the tradeoff between risk and return. Over the long-term the greater the risk the greater the expected return with risk generally defined as the volatility of returns over time. An investment that has the potential for its returns to deviate greatly from the expected average return will be considered risky while an investment with a return profile that differs very little from the expected average will be considered low risk. The assumption is that the volatility of returns is evenly distributed so that actual returns are expected to be above expectations half of the time and below expectations half of the time. In addition, the likelihood that returns will greatly exceed expectations in a given year is assumed to be the same as the likelihood that the returns will fall well below expectations which may include years with large losses. This symmetry of returns around the expected average forms the foundation of the arithmetic models that are used to calculate risk. The problem is there are a number of factors that make investment returns, and thus wealth creation, asymmetrical so that the actual level of risk for an investment strategy is often understated.

Stock market returns do not always fall into the symmetrical pattern assumed by the risk models. One can simply compare the actual returns to those that would be predicted using a standard distribution. While the standard distribution assumes that returns are symmetrical the actual results shows that they can differ from the assumed pattern.

S&P 500 Annual Returns 1970-2017

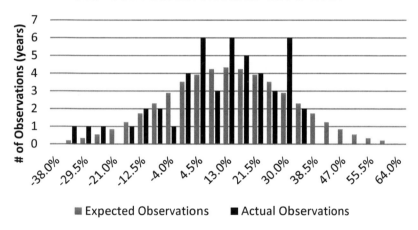

Source: Standard and Poor's

The previous chart shows the number of years that the S&P 500 posted returns within several ranges. The grey bars show the expected number of years the returns would fall within a given range while the black bars show the number of years that returns actually fell within that range. For example, the symmetrical pattern would predict that returns would fall within a few percent of 8.8% on average 4.25 times but the actual number was just 3 and it predicts the number of times that returns would fall within a few percent of 30% is just 3 but the actual number of observations was 6. In other words, the normal symmetrical distribution assumed by the statistical models is often not an accurate reflection of real-world results.

Since 1970 the actual returns have been skewed to the left side of the curve showing more years with lower, or even negative returns, than the symmetrical standard distribution predicts. In fact, of the 48 annual observations 20 were above average, 6 were in-line with the average and 22 were below average. In addition, as the chart shows, many of the returns below the average were large losses including declines of 22%, 26%, and 37%. It is also important to note that a large number of observations fall near the average with half between 0% and 21%. This pattern of a small number of large annual losses and a large number of smaller incremental gains has led to the saying: "The stock market typically goes up the stairs but down the elevator."

The asymmetrical pattern of returns can have a big impact on the total wealth generated because when investment returns are compounded from year to year the losses have a greater negative impact than the gains have a positive impact. For example, an investment that increases in value by 50% in the first year and decreases in value by 50% in the second year has an average annual rate of return of 0%. However, the compounded return is -25% over the two years or -13.40% per year ($100 increased by 50% equals a balance of $150. If the $150 then loses 50% it will fall to $75, a 25% loss over two years). The effect is the same no matter the order of the returns. This shows how losses can have a much greater impact than the gains, so it requires an even larger gain to offset a loss. Therefore, the asymmetry of investment returns can lead to an even greater asymmetry in wealth creation over time as the wealth outcomes are skewed to the downside. For this reason, the risk of a loss of wealth is greater than what is captured by the risk and return statistics which are a compilation of one-year returns rather than a reflection of the change in wealth from compounded returns. This asymmetry in returns and wealth creation partly explain why the loss of wealth during market downturns can be greater than many expect.

Taxes may also contribute to the asymmetry of wealth creation. When returns are realized in a non-retirement investment account the income is subject to taxation. Interest and short-term capital gains are taxed at ordinary income tax rates while qualified dividends and long-term capital gains are taxed at a lower preferential rate. The tax paid reduces the amount of wealth that is generated from positive investment returns. Meanwhile, when an investor loses money on an investment they are still required to pay taxes on their interest and dividends while their losses are limited to $3,000 per tax year. In other words, when investments produce gains all of the gains are subject to taxation. But when investments decline in value, the amount of loss that can be used to reduce the investor's tax liability is capped at just $3,000 which may be a small fraction of the amount lost. So, the investor gets to keep only a portion of their gains but must incur almost all of the loses.

The estate tax can also contribute to the asymmetry of wealth creation. An investor with total wealth near the estate tax exemption equivalent ($11.2 million per person in 2018) has a skewed wealth creation distribution. If the individual grows their wealth at a rate faster than inflation the additional wealth may be subject to a federal estate tax of 40%. However, if an investment performs poorly and the investor loses money they will take all of the loss. So, the wealth creation distribution creates a scenario where the investor's estate gets to keep 60% of their gains but loses 100% of the losses. The $11.2 million per person threshold may seem too high for most people to worry about but it should be noted that many US states have estate tax regimes that tax estates that exceed $1 million to $2 million and have tax rates as high as 15-20%. Therefore, even those with more modest estates in states that have an estate tax may be subject to a skewed wealth creation distribution in which the gains are limited by taxes but the losses are not offset by deductions or a reduced tax bill.

Finally, the wealth distribution is skewed by the law of diminishing marginal utility. Utility is an economics term that refers to the usefulness or enjoyment that an individual gets from an item, in this case money. The idea behind diminishing marginal utility is that money becomes less valuable to an individual the more that they accumulate. If an individual has no money the first dollar that they receive will be very valuable as it will allow them to buy something to eat. The second dollar will also be very valuable as it may allow for a larger meal but it will not be as valuable as the first dollar. This relationship continues with each additional dollar being less and less valuable than the dollars that came before. That is why an additional $10,000 will mean fairly little to a billionaire while it would be considered a wonderful windfall for a family making $70,000 per year. The law of diminishing marginal utility means the utility generated from gains in wealth is skewed so that losses are viewed more negatively than gains of an equal amount are viewed positively. In other words, the losses hurt more than the gains help.

The asymmetry of wealth creation should be considered when creating a financial or investment plan. Investors must factor in the impact that compounding returns, taxes, and diminishing utility are likely to have when determining how much risk to take in the pursuit of returns. While big gains can be exciting the actual increase in wealth may be much less than realized. Meanwhile, the losses that may appear from time to time are often more painful than an equal amount in gains as they may not be reduced by tax savings leaving the investor to bear the full brunt of the loss.

17

Planning Assumptions

Financial planners love to use the quote attributed to Benjamin Franklin that "failing to plan is planning to fail." While this quote can be quite accurate when it comes to finances it does not capture the entire essence of what it means to plan. Dwight D. Eisenhower said "... plans are useless, but planning is indispensable." Both quotes stress the importance of planning for the future. However, the Eisenhower quote highlights that the plan is not the important part. It's the planning process that is most important.

Planning for the future is always a difficult endeavor. The future is inherently unknown and unknowable. Therefore, assumptions must be made about a number of key variables. In finance these variables include the level of interest rates, the rate of inflation, investment risk premiums (excess return from incurring risk), market volatility, currency exchange rates, correlations between different investments (the degree to which prices move together or independently), and tax rates among others. Attempting to accurately predict all of these variables is akin to trying to predict the World Series winners for the next 20 years. It may be possible to get some years correct but some years the prediction is likely to be wildly off the mark.

The key to the planning process is to not just make assumptions but to test the assumptions. Assume one believes that inflation will average 3%, in-line with the long-term historical average, for the next 20 years. What would happen if inflation rates were higher than expected, say an average of 6% for the next 20 years? What would that mean for the plan and how can that risk be mitigated? Or what if market volatility is elevated in the future? What actions could be taken to adapt the plan to such an environment? It is important to think through these scenarios ahead of time by questioning assumptions and anticipating forecasting errors in order to identify and manage risks.

This highlights the importance of flexibility. A plan must be flexible enough to be able to adapt to a future in which reality may differ, sometimes greatly, from the original assumptions. A plan that is too ridged, built for one type of economic, financial, or market environment, will be broken by changing trends, unanticipated economic dislocations, or financial market upheavals. A plan must be able to change in response to changes in economic, financial, and market conditions.

Currently, many plans are being implemented with assumptions that in hindsight may appear foolish. Many expect stock market returns going forward to be in-line with past returns despite stock prices trading at historically high levels compared to measures of value such as earnings, sales, and cash flows. In addition, some expect bond market returns to be in-line with past experiences despite interest rates, the largest contributor to bond returns, being near historical lows. Others expect portfolios that are balanced between stocks and bonds to provide a moderate risk/return profile despite central bank intervention increasing the correlation between stock and bond returns which may increase the risk of losses when that support is withdrawn. It is important to ask what assumptions are a reflection of the current environment rather than a rational assessment of the future and its many possible outcomes.

The reason the planning process is so valuable is that it requires thinking. To create a plan one must consider different courses of action. The optimal course will depend on many variables that at the time of planning will be unknown. By considering multiple scenarios ahead of time an individual may be able to alter their course quickly and effectively should their assumptions prove to be flawed. This adaptability and the contingency plans that come with it are the real benefit from creating a financial plan.

18

Probabilities and the Unexpected

How often does an unlikely event make headlines? In a world that is often defined by statistics the unlikely seems to be increasingly common. Just open a newspaper, or access the online equivalent, and unlikely events regularly top the page. In geopolitical news, events that even the most informed analysts assigned a low probability often occur taking global leaders by surprise. The sports page regularly contains stories of improbable upsets and teams or athletes achieving what was previously believed to be impossible feats. Even the weather page contains examples of Mother Nature's propensity to confound statistical models. Of course, the financial page is no different as events should only occur once every hundred years or so that from a statistical standpoint seem to occur every few decades. This is not to say that the statistical models are wrong (although in some cases they are) but rather to point out that unlikely events occur quite frequently in one form or another. It is important to remember that even events that are very unlikely to occur are not impossible, just improbable, so they will occur on occasion. When everything is measured something that was deemed improbable is likely to occur quite often simply due to the large amount of data being analyzed.

For example, assume a statistical model examines a data set and estimates that an event has a one-in-a-million probability of occurring. If one million such data sets are tracked daily a one-in-a-million event will occur on average once per day. So even though the probability of such events are low they will occur regularly due to the large amount of data sets monitored. The difficultly lies not in determining whether such improbable events will occur but rather where they will occur.

The issue in many cases is not the statistical models but rather human perception. Humans have a tendency to think of improbable events as being impossible or at least as being far less likely than they actually are. This tendency makes a lot of sense from a practical standpoint. If people were constantly worried about low probability events, such as being hit by a meteor or struck by lightning, it would be difficult to live productive lives. So most people shrug off such possibilities and go on with their day. However, when it comes to risk management it is important to remember that just because something hasn't happened before, or has not happened for a long time, does not mean it can't happen. An event that is impossible can be ignored. An event that is merely improbable cannot be.

The reason that the difference between a low probability and zero probability event is important is that it has a big impact on the math that is used to assess the risk. One way to do this is to multiply the potential cost should the event occur by the likelihood of it occurring. So the cost of a zero probability event (assuming the risk was properly assessed) will always be zero no matter how large the potential cost. On the other hand, a low probability event, such as an individual's home burning down, has a non-zero probability and a high cost. If the probability of the home burning down were one-percent per year and the cost to replace the home and its contents were $400,000, the potential cost per year would be $4,000 ($400,000 times one percent). If an individual assumes this low probability event is a zero probability event it could lead to financial ruin should the home burn down with no insurance coverage. On the other hand, if the risk is properly assessed as a non-zero probability the individual should be willing to pay to transfer or hedge the risk in order to avoid the risk of financial ruin. Using this example, the individual may be willing to pay up to $4,000 per year for homeowners' insurance to transfer the financial risk of their home being destroyed by fire to an insurance company.

This is especially important in the financial world where low probability events are actually more common than most statistical models predict. In addition, there are a plethora of low probability risks that when combined increase the risk of a financial shock occurring even if they are individually unlikely. For example, during the financial crisis a highly rated investment bank and insurance company failed, US Treasury bills paid a negative interest rate, and stock prices fluctuated wildly beyond what statistical models estimated possible. Not to mention the Flash Crash in 2010, the Taper Tantrum in 2013, and the spike in the volatility index in early 2018. These are all extremely low probability events that occurred during periods of economic stress and during periods of stable economic growth. As the previous examples show there are many different risk factors that may impact the financial markets at any given time. Many of these may be low probability events, but there are a large number of them that must be considered, so an unlikely event can occur anytime and without warning. Therefore, it is important to attempt to identify these risks, assess their probability of occurring, and then take action to hedge, transfer, or avoid those risks. Ignoring risks and hoping for the best is not a viable long-term investment strategy.

Low probability events also impact other areas of financial planning. For example, there is a low probability that an individual will die or become disabled during their working years. However, this probability is not zero so it should not be ignored. Fortunately, because the probability is low, the financial risk of death or disability can be transferred to an insurance company at a relatively low cost. The key is to recognize the possibility of such an event and include it in a risk management plan.

In addition, many people delay creating an estate plan in preparation of their own death or incapacity. It is true that the risk of an individual dying or becoming incapacitated in a given year is low which makes it easy to put off planning. However, while the risk may be low the cost of failing to plan can be quite high. This makes it important to take this risk seriously and plan accordingly by taking action to avoid it. For example, this risk can be avoided by paying an attorney to create an estate plan. The cost of creating an estate plan may be much lower than the cost of not having a plan making it a good financial tradeoff.

Finally, the risk of being audited by the tax authorities in a given year is fairly low. Yet the IRS conducts over one million audits each year so the probability is clearly greater than zero. While the risk of an audit may be low, the cost can be substantial in the form of additional tax, interest, and penalties. For this reason, it is important to address this risk by seeking competent tax advice, maintaining proper records, and avoiding inaccurate or excessive deductions. This may come at a small cost in terms of time and money, but it may be worth it to reduce the risk of a costly audit.

Unlikely events will occur, but it is impossible to determine when or how. Turning a blind eye to the risk of improbable events will not make them go away or make them less likely to occur. Therefore, it is important to plan accordingly by assessing and addressing these risks.

19

Extrapolation, Contrarianism, and Analysis

Forecasts and projections are an important part of financial planning and financial analysis. Typically, assumptions about the future are made, statistical tools are applied, and conclusions are drawn in an effort to better understand future possibilities and probabilities. But not all forecasts are created equal.

Businesses use forecasts in the form of pro forma financial statements to plan for the future. Financial analysts use models to create earnings projections for the companies that they follow. Economists use economic constructs to forecast economic data. These all serve an important role in helping to understand the financial world and inform decisions about the future. The problem often arises when these forecasts and projections are not based on suitable analysis but instead are based on extrapolations or contrarianism.

An extrapolation is simply the continuation of a recent trend into the future. When a series of data points has been trending upward an extrapolation will predict that they will continue to do so. On the other hand, if a downward trend is in place an extrapolation will forecast a further decline.

Often an extrapolation is the safe prediction for a professional to make. People's expectations are influenced by recent events so an extrapolation may be in-line with the expectations of many observers. In addition, trends can be a powerful force that often picks up momentum as they persist due to a tendency for people to change their behavior in response to a perceived pattern in the data. For example, when housing prices increase a greater number of potential homeowners, fueled by a fear of missing out, may rush to buy further bidding up prices. This can cause a trend to persist for far longer than most would believe possible.

There is also a tendency for individuals to use extrapolation to make bold predictions in an effort to gain attention. For example, in 1999 there was a book published called *Dow 36,000*, which was quite a bold prediction, considering the Dow Jones Industrial Average had just passed the 10,000 level. This book was soon eclipsed by the next best seller titled *Dow 100,000*. Yet today, nearly 20 years later, the Dow only sits at approximately 25,000. In retrospect it is obvious that this was the result of the extrapolation of a trend to an absurd extent. However, most economic and financial data is cyclical (see Cycles) so most trends eventually end. This can make forecasts based on the extrapolation of recent events very damaging when a cycle eventually shifts from one phase to the next.

Likewise, contrarianism can also be dangerous. Contrarianism is a tendency to predict a reversal in an existing trend. Often economic and market commentators will predict the end of a trend to stand out from the crowd and thus attract more attention to their prediction. Contrarians know that eventually most trends end when cyclical forces take over so there is a high probability that they will eventually be proven right. However, it can take years before a persistent trend may reverse, which can make constant contrarianism a weak form of forecasting.

For example, there were a number of academics and market commentators that predicted the end of the housing boom years before it actually occurred. When these predictions proved correct they were heralded as master prognosticators in the media. Yet their predictions were of little practical use given the long delay between the initial prediction and the eventual result. This is especially problematic when predictions are made about cyclical factors that have a long-term upward bias. A contrarian may predict a market downturn but if it does not occur for years to come the correction may only offset a portion of the gains made since the initial prediction. Therefore, despite correctly calling a decline, the prices may still be higher than they were when the prediction was made giving it little value.

It is important to identify the forecasts and predictions that are based on extrapolation or contrarianism as opposed to a balanced analysis of the facts and circumstances. This requires a detailed review of the assumptions made and the mathematical or statistical tools used to draw the conclusions. If the assumptions are biased or the quantitative tools are designed to produce a specific conclusion the results should be taken with a grain of salt. On the other hand, if the analysis draws on reasonable assumptions and uses appropriate mathematical and statistical tools it may be worth taking into consideration.

Naturally, all forecasts and predictions are subject to an error rate as the future is inherently unknowable. Therefore, even the most robust analysis should not be relied upon too heavily. Risk management tools should be implemented to manage and minimize the level of damage that may be done should any forecast or prediction prove to be incorrect.

20

Wealth Equation

Some people believe that the purpose of investing is to amass wealth. The idea is simple. You invest your money, it is allocated in some way or another, and the end result following a sufficiently long time horizon is wealth. This process can be summed up in a tidy little equation: Investing x ? = Wealth.

Unfortunately, in the real world things are not so simple. The real purpose of investing is to supply capital (money) to the productive endeavors that advance society. For example, investing in the stock of a growing company that produces products or services that are in high demand will benefit society by allowing the company to invest to meet the growing demand. Or lending money by purchasing a mortgage bond may benefit society by providing the money needed to help increase the rate of home ownership. The incentive for these and other similar activities is the potential for wealth. In other words, the ? in the Investing x ? = Wealth equation matters. It matters a lot.

The question mark (?) can take many forms. It could be Investing x Technology Stock IPO in 1999 = $0 or Investing x Rental Home in 2006 = - Wealth. On the other hand, it could be Investing x US Stock Market in

2009 = Increased Wealth. The point is that the ? is a multiplier that can be positive or negative and which determines the outcome: success and wealth or failure and losses.

Like any other commodity capital (investment dollars) is highly valued when it is scarce and little valued when it is plentiful. When risks are evident and uncertainty is high people want to hold on to their money for security. Thus, capital becomes scarce and its price (in this case potential returns) become elevated to entice people to invest. When risks are less evident and uncertainty has given way to complacency the supply of capital is abundant as people seek to grow their wealth rather than protect it. In this environment the price of capital (prospective future returns) is typically low as investors compete to deploy capital to the limited number of investment options.

For example, assume an investor is analyzing the stock of XYZ, Inc. It is impossible to know what price the stock will trade at in 10 years but for arguments sake assume it is $100 per share. After all, the price in the future is fixed, even if cannot be known in advance. If the investor were able to hop into a time machine and go 10 years into the future there would be only one price. Price estimates may change between now and then but those are just estimates of what that future price may be. So an investor that pays $50 for the stock would earn an average annual return of 7.2% per year over the following 10 year period ($50 growing to $100 over 10 years). Meanwhile, an investor that pays $60 per share will earn just 5.2% per year ($60 growing to $100 over 10 years). The higher price, a result of a greater supply of capital, the lower the prospective return.

The one constant is risk. Risk comes from the misallocation of capital to a purpose that is unproductive. For example, funding a biotech start-up with a new drug that does not pass clinical trials and therefore makes it to market may be an unproductive investment in the end. In this case the new drug will not benefit society and there will be no wealth created or allocated to those who provided the capital to fund the drug's development. Similarly, buying a condo as an investment property in an already over-saturated market creates little, if any, value. The purpose of a condo is to provide shelter at an affordable cost. If there isn't anyone who needs shelter, or if those who do need shelter cannot afford the rents required to make the condo a viable investment, the condo will have little benefit to society and therefore is unlikely to be a source of wealth until demand increases to the point where the condo offers value.

Risk persists over time. The misallocation of capital can occur in good times and bad. However, in good times the perception of risk is often too low causing investors to give opportunities too little scrutiny. This can increase the likelihood of capital being misallocated.

In addition, during good times when investment prices are high the prospective returns on good investments are often too low to offset the potential losses on poor investments. Therefore, even the risk-managing characteristics of diversification can be limited. For example, having half of a portfolio allocated to bonds yielding 4% interest will do little to offset losses if the other half is allocated to stocks that decline 50%. In other words, when investment prices are high the reward for properly allocating capital is diminished while the punishment for failing to properly allocate capital is enhanced.

Risk is also a function of expectations. Financial markets price-in future expectations. High growth expectations lead to higher future stock price estimates which lead to higher current prices. But what happens when the growth expectations are too high? Future stock price estimates and thus current stock prices may exceed levels that will produce future wealth. So risk is a constant but the reward for accepting risk fluctuates with prices, the opportunities available, and expectations for the future. How does an investor navigate the financial markets under these circumstances? The key is to be an independent thinker and avoid common mistakes. These mistakes include:

• Believing that rising or falling prices are an accurate predictor of the future prospects of an investment. Prices often rise too high or fall too low based on investor psychology and therefore may deviate from a rational assessment of an investment's future prospects (see The Often Irrational Nature of Prices).

• When there are few attractive investment opportunities available there is no rule that says an investor must stay in the game. When the reward for winning is to too small to offset the potential risk of losing then sitting on the sidelines may be the best option.

• Don't adopt the expectations of others, especially when they are abnormally high or low compared to historical norms. Following the herd may feel safe but can be dangerous when the herd is running in the wrong direction.

21

The Often Irrational Nature of Prices

Prices are a peculiar thing. Price signals, the information consumers and investors derive from changes in prices, are an important determinant of consumer and investor behavior. Yet these signals are often misunderstood as they can appear irrational at times or may seem to send contradictory messages. This makes prices an important piece of the economic and financial puzzle when they are examined to decipher the signal that they are conveying.

In economics prices are determined by the equilibrium where the supply curve crosses the demand curve. In other words, a price is the point where buyers and sellers, both acting in their own self-interest, choose to engage in a transaction. When the supply or demand curve shifts due to a change in buyers' or sellers' attitudes, perceptions, or circumstances, prices adjust quickly to the new equilibrium where trade can once again take place. This makes for a tidy theory but in real life the picture is far more complicated sometimes leading to peculiar behavior which must be incorporated into the economic and financial analysis of prices.

For example, there is the frenzied consumerism that a sale can trigger. Low prices, or in some cases prices that are not low but are perceived to be low, can trigger a feeding frenzy that makes piranha look tame by comparison. Low prices can cause consumers to ignore important factors, like quality, that determine the value derived from a transaction. In addition, low prices can cause some consumers to ignore high non-monetary transaction costs such as waiting in line for hours before a store opens or going from store to store in an attempt to find a discounted item still in stock. Clearly, when prices are low it can cause unusual consumer behavior. However, to a degree it does make sense that prices below the equilibrium price, where demand would be expected to overwhelm supply, would cause unusual activity.

What is odd is that at other times low prices have the opposite effect. A price that is too low can send a signal that a product or service is of low-quality causing consumers to avoid it. If it seems too good to be true then it probably is, they may reason. The trick is that sometimes this is an accurate assessment and sometimes it is not. In fact, there are multiple stories of products and services that were failures when marketed at low prices but were salvaged and even thrived when the price was increased. Why would consumers avoid the product at a low price but seek it out when it is sold at a high price? How can a low price send one signal under one set of circumstances and a different signal under another set of circumstances?

It is not just low prices that can cause consumers to behave oddly. For example, some people choose to buy high priced goods and services purely because they are highly priced. Economists call this conspicuous consumption. People choose to spend lavishly on certain brand name items to send a message to others that they can afford such luxury. Of course, it is all fine and good if wealthy people choose to overspend to show off their wealth but many people who cannot afford high priced luxury items will still pay a premium price for them in order to feel or appear wealthier than they are. In other words, instead of high prices causing a decrease in demand it can actually create its own demand because of the high price.

Then there are the oddities studied by behavioral finance practitioners. For example, the endowment effect states that an individual will assign a greater value to an item after they possess it than before. Once someone owns something they demand a higher price to part with it than they were willing to pay to acquire it. This violates the rules of the equilibrium price where supply meets demand as the same person is willing to supply an item at one price but demands it at different price.

Prices can also create their own expectations. For example, inflation, which is a major determinate of prices, is primarily driven by inflation expectations and inflation expectations are largely driven by past inflation rates. This can create a cycle whereby inflation (higher prices) leads to increased inflation expectations which in turn leads to higher inflation and so on. The expectation of higher prices in the future can cause consumers to rush to buy at the lower current price bidding up prices in the process. The opposite can also be true. Deflation (falling prices) can cause consumers to defer expenditures as much as possible causing an oversupply of goods and services that pushes prices down further.

Prices can also move in anticipation of upcoming events. Investment prices often move before earnings announcements, the release of economic data, and interest rate announcements to the point where the stock market is considered a leading economic indicator. This can be interpreted as a form of speculation about the future. However, the speculation is not always correct which can sometimes lead to wild price swings over just a few days, hours, or even minutes. So prices can move based on the expectation that past observations will persist in the future as well as in anticipation of future changes in economic and financial factors.

Then there is the most powerful price factor of them all: the trend. A trend can start for a variety of reasons or even due to the culmination of a combination of factors. Either way, once a trend picks up steam it can gather momentum until it pushes prices higher or lower than most would have imagined possible beforehand. We have seen this play out in stock prices, real estate values, commodity prices and many other markets. The problem is that trends eventually reverse. This makes a trend similar to a campfire, the hotter it burns the more important it is to monitor to avoid disaster.

With prices containing so much information and affected by many, sometimes conflicting, factors how does one make sense of it all? The key is to understand that prices are important, but they are not the most important thing. Value is most important. It's less about what you pay and more about what you are getting for the price paid. A business has a value based on the earnings it can generate, real estate has a value based on its ability to provide shelter, and commodities have a value based on long-term supply and demand factors. The price may deviate from this value for a variety of reasons, but the value will act as an anchor does to a ship by pulling it back toward equilibrium. Therefore, long-term investors should focus on value to determine where the anchor lies below the surface, then observe the price to determine which direction and how hard the winds of the markets are blowing.

22

Prices, Values, and Volatility

O ne of the primary purposes of financial markets is to determine prices. Buyers and sellers are brought together and matched up at the prices at which they are willing to engage in a transaction. Once a transaction is complete the price is posted. This price is then used to determine the value of all other holdings. For example, if 100 shares of XYZ corporation trades at $100 per share then all other shares will be valued at $100 even if XYZ corporation has a million, or even a billion, shares outstanding. In truth, while the value may be $100 per share not everyone will be able to sell at the assigned value as it would take a large number of buyers willing to transact at that price. Therefore, values should be taken as an estimate of what an investment may be sold for rather than a hard and fast number, especially when an individual owns a large quantity that they may want to sell.

The impact of recent prices on values may be best demonstrated in the real estate market. Assume there are two identical homes located next to each other in the same neighborhood. If one sells, the price will be used to determine the value of the other both by certified appraisers and internet sites. Yet most people know to take those values as a suggestion of the actual value as a buyer must be found which can take months and may involve a lengthy negotiating process. If a seller is motivated to sell they may be forced to lower the price to find a buyer more quickly in which case they will realize a lower value. When a seller is under duress and there are few buyers at the time the price may be lowered substantially causing the values of nearby homes to drop sharply.

The same principles apply to other markets. If distressed sellers attempt to sell their stock at a time when there are few buyers they must accept lower and lower prices to do so. The decline in the value of the investment may cause other holders to attempt to sell pushing prices even lower. The uncertainty over the eventual price may cause buyers to sit on the sidelines allowing prices to fall further. This can occur due to negative news about an investment, in response to unsubstantiated rumors, or for no ascertainable reason whatsoever. Meanwhile, at any given time the majority of the owners of the investment may have no desire or intention to sell. Yet it only takes one buyer and one seller to engage in a transaction that causes the price to fall wiping out a large amount of investor value.

For example, on May 6, 2010 the US stock market declined sharply in an episode later labeled the Flash Crash. The decline in the markets wiped out over $1 trillion of investment value with the stocks of large, stable corporations selling for as little as one penny during the day. The most interesting part is that the crash has been blamed on a single trader who entered erroneous sell orders which then triggered a cascade of additional sell orders. The lack of buyers willing to step in and buy during the market freefall caused prices to crater. Many companies sold at prices that even the most pessimistic analysts would consider absurdly low. Yet there was no real fundamental news or meaningful event that changed the market landscape from the previous day.

This is how an imbalance between buyers and sellers can lead to price volatility. The volatility may lead to increased uncertainty about the future price which may cause further price volatility. In turn the change in prices will cause investment values to fluctuate, sometimes wildly, in the short-term. The key is to determine if the short-term change in prices is due to a longer-term change in the fundamental value of an investment or due to either buyers or sellers gaining a temporary advantage in the daily supply and demand tug-of-war.

So how does an individual protect themselves from the periods of high price volatility that occur every few years? Generally, there are two reasons that people are hurt by market price volatility. The first is that they are forced to sell when prices are down and therefore must accept the low prices being offered. For example, stock market prices tend to be low during economic recessions. Often during recessions many households experience reduced income due to high levels of unemployment, reduced work hours, etc. This combination of lower household income and lower stock prices can force households to sell stocks at low prices to supplement their cash flow to get through the difficult financial period. This can be avoided through proper risk management and diversification. The goal should be to allocate enough money to lower-risk investments to allow the household to get through the next economic downturn without needing to sell risky assets. If there are sufficient low-risk assets that can be sold to cover a household's cash flow needs during a recession the riskier investments can be held until the recession abates and their value recovers. This strategy can make a stock market or economic downturn a small setback that can be overcome within a few years rather than an event that requires a rethinking of an individual's long-term financial plan.

The second way that price volatility can damage a long-term financial plan is related to investor psychology. Some investors may have a strategy in place to deal with a market downturn but are still unable to psychologically handle the losses, especially when the financial markets seemingly post losses every day for several weeks or months or decline in value rapidly in a short time period. This can lead to financial stress which may cause some investors to sell risky assets, even though they do not need to, to stop the psychological discomfort that comes from watching their net worth decline. One way to avoid making this mistake is to focus on an asset's value rather than its price. Asset prices can change quickly due to market dynamics or the number of buyers and sellers in the market at any given moment. The long-term value of an asset changes very slowly over time based on a variety of factors that are longer-term in nature. For example, stock prices may decline sharply due to an expectation that an economic slowdown will cause corporate earnings to decline in the short-term. Yet the long-term value, which is based on multi-year or multi-decade earnings growth trends, will change very little. By focusing on this long-term value investors may find it psychologically easier to continue to hold risky assets when their prices are down. This will give markets an opportunity to normalize and allow prices to revert to a level that is closer to their estimated long-term value.

23

Mosaic Approach

Pompeii is an ancient Roman city that was buried in volcanic ash 2000 years ago. A large portion of the city has been uncovered giving some insight into life in an ancient Roman city. Among the many treasures that were uncovered during the excavation are a number of surprisingly well-preserved mosaics. One is a mosaic of a dog located in the entry way to the ruins of a large villa. The tour guides joke that it was the Roman equivalent of a "Beware of Dog" sign. Other mosaics were not so well preserved. Some are missing tiles or the colors are faded making it difficult to make out the picture. In those cases, it takes some imagination to decipher the message the mosaic was intended to convey. In other cases, the mosaics are in such bad shape that no amount of imagination can accurately fill in the gaps. More pieces to the puzzle (more tiles placed in the proper location) are needed to interpret the message.

In finance many analysts use an approach called the mosaic method. The idea is that every economic, financial, and market data point is a piece of a larger picture just as every tile adds to a mosaic. The more data that conforms to the same theme, the greater the clarity, and thus the greater the analyst's confidence in their projections for the future. When the data contradicts itself the picture becomes hazy leading to reduced confidence in the projections. Of course, much like archaeologists who struggle to fill in the gaps when tiles are missing from a mosaic, financial analysts must also deal with blank spots where data is unavailable, too difficult to make-out, or too expensive to obtain. These blank areas require some imagination to figure out how the unknown data may fit into the picture. The way in which these unknowns are interpreted, either optimistically or pessimistically, can be a large influence on an investment manager's philosophy and strategy.

The mosaic method rarely shows a unified picture of the markets. Even when the picture looks bright there are often some dim areas around the edges which reflect the potential risks to the outlook. At other times the picture can be quite bleak with some glimmers of hope around the edges. But these scenarios are typically quite rare. Most often the picture is a mix of opportunities and risks.

Periods where the picture is mixed are quite challenging for analysts using the mosaic method. For example, by late 2017 the bulk of the picture, a combination of economic, financial, and market data, was darkening. Many measures of stock market valuations were well above their historical average signaling that stocks may be overpriced. Household debt in the US was hitting a new high, even eclipsing the levels set before the financial crisis in 2008-09. Short-term interest rates were rising as the Federal Reserve withdrew the stimulus injected into the financial system during the previous crisis. However, there was a portion of the picture that was bright and full of anticipation. Consumer confidence and business sentiment were at high levels following the passage of the first major tax reform in over 30 years. Housing prices were rising and retail spending was strong even if it was primarily fueled by consumer borrowing.

Investors appeared to focus only on the optimistic data points while ignoring the remainder of the picture. For this reason, market returns were in-line with what one would expect when the picture looks much brighter. Stock prices surged in January 2018 making it the best start to a year in many decades. The result was that prices moved more and more out of line with the facts and circumstances that dictate prices over the long-term. Given the cyclical nature of the economy and financial markets this is not the first time that investors focused on the positives while ignoring the negatives, nor will it be the last. Unfortunately, history has shown that the aftermath of such periods of excessive optimism often do not work out well for the majority of investors.

Such an environment has three major implications. The first is that it may limit the number of tools that investors choose to use. When the average investor is only focused on the few factors that seem to be driving market returns then only the tools related to those factors will be useful to make sense of market movements. For example, when prices become detached from fundamentals then analysts may rely on trend analysis, relative valuation (investment values compared to other investments rather than on a stand-alone basis), and relative strength (an investment's performance compared to its peers or the market as a whole). A reliance on fewer tools emphasizes the drawbacks of those tools rather than allowing for a more holistic approach to risk assessment and management. In other words, investors choose to ignore the big picture and focus only on the data points that conform with recent market performance. This can be a dangerous strategy when investors come to their senses and realize that market values are not supported by the bulk of the data.

The second implication is some investors may decide to take preemptive measures to reduce/manage risk. This requires an assessment of future risk and return opportunities to determine the cost/benefit of a more defensive strategy. The cost/benefit analysis should include the potential cost of foregone returns in the short-term and the estimated benefits which may be derived from reducing the volatility of returns. This often leads to making incremental changes over time rather than taking the timing risk of making a large change all at once. The incremental approach can be a good strategy for investors with a long-term time horizon. It will cause them to reduce risk when market prices are surging but the economic and financial picture is darkening. This may allow an investor to take advantage of the high prices by taking profits while still maintaining a risk profile that is in-line with their long-term strategy.

The third implication is that it creates anxiety for many investment professionals. The mosaic method forces investment professionals to regularly update the data that makes up each tile in the mosaic. When more and more of the data turns negative but market prices continue to trend upward it can create high levels of stress, especially for those who have seen this pattern play out in the past. This anxiety may cause investment professionals to move to a more defensive strategy to reduce the risk of a decline in prices.

The last 11 months of 2018 is a great example of how a disconnect between market performance and the market fundamentals highlighted using the mosaic approach often plays out. The markets not only gave back the strong gains from January 2018 but actually slipped into negative territory shortly after reaching the January high and posted a negative return for all of 2018. The economy did not slip into recession during this time period and there was no financial crisis or other major economic or market shock. The market simply declined because prices exceeded that which could be justified by the bulk of the data. Investors who use the mosaic approach to track the economic and market climate may have been aware of this and taken steps to reduce the impact of a market decline on their investments. Those who chose to focus only on the factors that were driving the short-term market performance in late 2017 and early 2018 while ignoring the big picture were likely not as well positioned for the decline in prices that followed.

This is just one example, but it highlights the benefits of a disciplined adherence to the mosaic approach. It can be easy to become overly optimistic and seek out confirming evidence when the market is trending upward. Behavioral economists call this confirmation bias which is the tendency for people to seek out evidence that supports their existing opinions or the outcome that they seek. The mosaic approach is designed to combat this tendency by forcing individuals to take a broader set of facts and circumstances into account when making decisions. It will not allow investors to perfectly identify all of the periods of excessive market optimism or pessimism, but it is a valuable way to instill more discipline into the investment process.

24

Three Aspects to Risk

One of the first steps when creating an investment plan is to establish a risk target. This is often established through a personal interview, completing a risk questionnaire, or using an algorithm. The problem is that these methods generally hone in on just one aspect of risk which is how the investor feels about risk. Unfortunately, this is only part of the picture which can lead to an incomplete assessment of the ideal risk target. In fact, there are three different aspects of risk which need to be balanced to determine the proper risk target for an investor.

The first aspect of risk is the one which many investment managers focus on the most: An investor's willingness to take risk. An investor's willingness to take risk is a function of how they feel about risk. It comes down to their emotional reaction to changes in their investment values with an emphasis put on how they feel about a decline in values. Are they a risk-taker who feeds on the highs and lows of the market or do they lay awake at night when the markets are volatile? To what degree is their wiliness to take risk affected by the financial environment? Do they watch their accounts daily allowing anxiety to build with each decline or do they focus on the long-term and ignore short-term fluctuations? The link between an investor's emotional reaction to risk, which may change based on a variety of factors, and their willingness to take risk makes it the most volatile of the different aspects of risk. After all, an investor's emotional reaction to risk can change based on the market environment, their financial situation, the tone of reporting by the financial media, and how the people around them feel about investment risk. This can make an investor's willingness to take risk an inaccurate and ever changing way to assess their risk tolerance. Yet it is still important because an investor's willingness to take risk is a large determinate of whether they will stick to a long-term investment plan when the economy and financial markets hit a rough patch.

The second aspect of risk that should be assessed is an investor's ability to take risk. An investor's ability to take risk is largely a function of their financial situation and time horizon. If an investor does not have the money to cover their living expenses for the next three to six months they may not be in a position to put their savings at risk. In addition, if their savings may be needed in a financial emergency it may be best deposited into a savings vehicle, such as a bank money market account, rather than invested in riskier assets. On the other hand, an investor who has accumulated or inherited a large sum may have a high ability to take risk as any losses will have a limited impact on their financial well-being.

The time horizon for an investment is also important. Someone who is young and saving for retirement may have a high ability to take risk as the money will likely be invested for many years through multiple market cycles before it is needed. Meanwhile, an investor who has been saving money for a child's education expenses which will be needed in a few years may have a limited ability to take risk because a market downturn could jeopardize the end goal. Typically, a financial planner will help an investor to assess their ability to take risk by conducting a review of the investor's financial situation including their assets, liabilities, income, and expenses. The planner can then help the investor understand how their ability to take risk may differ from their willingness to take risk. The investor's ability to take risk should be viewed as their maximum risk level.

The third aspect of risk is an investor's need to take risk. Investment risk and expected return are linked. Therefore, if an investor takes too little risk they may not realize a high enough rate of return to achieve their financial goals. For example, an individual may need to achieve a 5% average annual rate of return to achieve their financial goals. In this case they need to take sufficient risk to have a reasonable expectation of achieving this rate of return. If they instead deposit their money into a certificate of deposit that is paying 4% per year they will be unlikely to achieve their goals because their risk level is too low to earn the required 5% return. The low risk level may result in little risk of financial loss but it may increase the risk that the individual will not achieve their long-term goals. The question that must be asked is: What is more important, avoiding short-term losses or avoiding the risk of falling short of long-term financial goals? When looking at the big picture, falling short of long-term goals can often be much more damaging to an individual's financial well-being.

Typically, the required rate of return can be determined by incorporating the financial resources that can be committed to a goal with the time horizon for achieving the goal and the expected volatility of returns. Financial models can be used to merge these factors and determine the risk and return level needed to achieve the goal. The need to take risk should be considered the minimum level of risk an investor should take.

One key to an effective investment plan is a risk target that balances all three aspects of risk. Of course, there will be times when the different aspects of risk are in conflict with each other requiring some action to bring them into alignment. When an investor's willingness to take risk is below their need and ability to take risk the solution may be to educate the investor about investment risk. Education may help the investor focus on the long-term path of the financial markets rather than short-term market fluctuations. It can also be useful to show that the real risk is the risk of falling short of achieving financial goals rather than the risk that the value on their investment statement may increase or decrease from month-to-month or year-to-year. The goal is to help the logical side of the investor's brain overcome the emotional side so they can increase their willingness to take risk to bring it in-line with their ability to take risk and need to take risk.

If the investor's willingness to take risk is above their ability and need to take risk the investor should be made aware of the benefits of a risk minimization approach (see Risk Maximization versus Risk Minimization) as it may be advisable to take less risk than they believe they can tolerate in order to increase the probability of achieving their goals. Another option is to carve out a portion of the investor's portfolio, which is not needed to fund their financial goals and therefore they have the ability to lose without creating financial distress, and allocate it to riskier investments. This can give the investor a portion of their portfolio to focus on to satisfy their emotional inclination to take risk without jeopardizing their financial goals.

If an investor's ability to take risk is below their willingness and need to take risk the investor may need to reassess their financial goals. Maybe their goals are too ambitious given their financial resources. Many people would love to retire early and spend a month out of every year on vacation in an exotic location but that does not mean it is feasible given limited financial resources and other financial responsibilities. So the financial goals must be within reach given reasonable assumptions about investment risks and returns. Financial planners can help investors understand the dangers of taking risks that exceed their ability to take risk and instead focus on more attainable financial goals.

When an investor's ability to take risk exceeds their willingness and need to take risk it can be beneficial to segment their investments into pools of money that will be used for different purposes. An investor with substantial financial resources may have a high ability to take risk but does not want or need to take such a high level of risk. Their high ability to take risk may be a sign that they have more than enough money to meet their financial needs over their lifetime. Therefore, the investor may benefit from carving out some of their investments and designate it as money that will be left as an inheritance, money that will be donated to charity, etc. The different pools of money may allow the investor to look at them differently and assign a different willingness to take risk to each. For example, money that is designated as inheritance for a child or grandchild can be invested more aggressively based on the beneficiaries' financial situation and time horizon. This approach could increase both the investor's willingness and need to take risk with a portion of their investments so that it is in-line with their ability to take risk.

Finally, if an investor's need to take risk exceeds their willingness and ability to take risk the investor may need to allocate more of their financial resources to funding the goal. For example, the investor may need to prioritize the goal over other financial goals and therefore allocate more of their savings to funding the goal so that the required rate of return is reduced to a more reasonable level. Another option is to reduce spending to free-up more money that can be saved and allocated to the goal in question. If an investor attempts to fund too many financial goals they may find that their financial resources are spread too thin to have a high probability of achieving all of their goals given reasonable investment risk and return assumptions. In this case, it may be beneficial to rank financial goals into top priorities and aspirational goals with the bulk of financial resources allocated to the top priorities and any excess funds allocated to the aspirational goals.

If an investor's need to take risk is below their willingness and ability to take risk they may want to explore what financial goals they may have which are not funded under their existing plan. Perhaps they want to take their family on vacation or fund their grandchildren's education. Adding these goals may increase their need to take risk but as long as it does not exceed their willingness or ability to take risk it should not create a problem. In addition, it may allow them to get more satisfaction from their financial resources over their lifetime.

25

Risk Management Priorities

R isk is a part of life. However, some risks can be managed. One risk management technique is risk avoidance such as avoiding risky behavior like cliff diving, paragliding, or bungie jumping. Other risks, such as some financial risks, can be transferred by purchasing insurance. Then there are the risks that must be accepted as a part of the human condition, such as the risk of a meteor hitting the Earth. Any risk that is not avoided or transferred is retained. Everyone must decide which risks they are willing to retain and which they are not. This often comes down to the type of insurance and the insurance limits that an individual chooses to purchase. Given that the financial resources available to purchase insurance are limited, the types of policies and their limits must be prioritized to allocate the portion of a household's budget that can be dedicated to insurance to the areas where it is most important. One way to do this is to take a life cycle view of risk in order to prioritize the types of insurance that are likely to be needed most.

When a person is born the most important insurance is health insurance. In fact, health insurance is the most important type of insurance throughout an individual's lifetime. Health insurance provides access to preventative health care (risk avoidance). It is also a way to avoid financial risk as not having health insurance has historically been one of the leading causes of personal bankruptcy. Therefore, not having health insurance can be one of the greatest financial risks that an individual can take.

Once a person reaches driving age and plans to operate a vehicle, auto insurance becomes the next priority. Not only is auto insurance with minimum liability limits required by state law but an accident without auto insurance could lead to a lawsuit and a financial judgment against the driver and/or vehicle owner.

The next milestone is typically when an individual reaches the age where they get a job and support themselves financially. At this age disability insurance becomes the second priority to health insurance. At a young age an individual is more likely to become disabled than to die. If they become disabled they could have a long lifetime ahead of them with no means to support themselves. Often disability insurance is available as an employee benefit either as a part of an employer paid benefits package or as an add-on that the employee can purchase. This can be a good place to start when exploring disability insurance options. However, it is advisable to consult a financial planner to determine the amount of coverage needed and to explore other options before committing to one provider.

Next an individual may choose to buy a home. Homeowner's insurance will then join auto insurance as the third priority as the loss of a home due to fire or a natural disaster could be a major financial setback. In addition, if the home is subject to a mortgage then homeowner's insurance will be required or the mortgage lender will add the expense of higher cost insurance to the mortgage payment.

When an individual has others dependent on their income, whether it is a spouse or children, life insurance moves up the priority list. The loss of a breadwinner can not only be emotionally devastating but also financially devastating to a household. Life insurance can be used to replace lost income and allow a household to pay the bills while they go through the grieving process. It can also be used to fund long-term financial commitments such as paying off a mortgage or funding children's college education. However, given the limited financial resources available to pay for insurance premiums it is important to avoid buying too much life insurance or purchasing high cost life insurance while neglecting to fund other insurance needs.

As an individual ages and their earning power increases they will likely accumulate assets including long-term savings. At this point liability insurance becomes a greater priority. When there are assets to protect from a lawsuit, liability insurance with sufficient coverage limits is an important form of protection from financial ruin. Therefore, it is important to pay close attention to the liability limits under auto and homeowner's insurance policies. If these coverage limits are insufficient given the insured's assets and income an excess liability or umbrella policy may be needed to extend the amount of liability coverage.

When an individual reaches retirement, life and disability insurance are often no longer a priority. Life and disability insurance are typically intended to replace an individual's income should they die or become disabled. If they have accumulated sufficient financial resources to be able to retire, they and their household are likely no longer dependent on their income, so life and disability insurance are no longer as important. However, longevity risk – the risk that an individual outlives their savings – becomes more important in retirement. There are some insurance products, such as annuities, that can be used to transfer this risk. However, these options often come at a high cost so retirees may choose to retain and manage this risk instead.

Finally, in retirement, long-term health care costs can become a larger risk. Long-term health care expenses can be quite high and can jeopardize most retirement plans. Long-term care insurance can be a way to transfer a portion of this risk to an insurance company in order to preserve retirement assets to pay for other expenses. It should be noted that the cost of long-term care insurance increases with age. Therefore, an individual may want to explore their options before retirement because securing a policy at a younger age may reduce the annual premium.

While risk cannot be eliminated it can be managed through an intelligent risk management plan. Often an important part of a risk management plan is the strategic use of insurance to transfer risks that have the potential to derail a financial plan. However, given the limited amount in a household budget to fund insurance premiums it is important to allocate the money to the highest priorities based on the insured's stage of life.

26

Avoid Financial Ruin

Games of chance are often used as metaphors for finance. Both involve and risk in an environment where the outcome is inherently uncertain. A successful gambler and a successful financial manager both rely heavily on mathematics and statistics to determine probabilities of success and failure, the returns and losses that are likely to result from a given strategy, and when risk-taking may be prudent and when it should be avoided. The big difference is that a gambler operates in a world that has a negative return bias whereas a financial manager has the expectation of a positive return bias. This means the probabilities are against the gambler as the edge goes to the house. If one gambles long enough they are likely to lose as the odds are against them. In contrast, the longer an investment manager's time frame the greater their chance of success. However, both must be adept at managing risk effectively in order to optimize their probability of success. In addition, both will agree that the most important part of risk management is to avoid the chance of ruin: The point at which everything is lost and the individual cannot continue to implement their strategy going forward.

A professional blackjack player knows that the odds are against them. However, they also know that there are points in the game where the odds change to be in their favor. For example, when the dealer is showing a 5 or a 6 there is the highest chance that the dealer will bust. Assuming the player has a hand that would be advantageous to double (double their bet but only get one additional card) or split (if the players first two cards are the same they can turn one hand into two by doubling the bet) the player may be able to increase their bet (increase their risk) when the odds are in their favor. Often these hands can be the difference between winning or losing money. The problem is that these situations do not come up very often. Therefore, a gambler must assess how much they will bet on each hand so that the house's edge does not wipe them out before they get an opportunity where the odds are in their favor. In addition, even when the odds are in the player's favor there is still a chance that they will not win so they cannot bet too much in these instances or they will increase the risk of ruin. On the other hand, if the player bets too little then their winnings when they are able to double their bet will not be large enough to change their result in a meaningful way. In addition, betting too little may allow them to stay in the game longer but the longer the time horizon the more likely that the odds will favor the house due to the negative return bias. A gambler cannot change the odds of the game but they can manage the risk by determining how much to bet on a given hand. Therefore, the gambler's risk management strategy will greatly influence their probability of success or failure.

Financial managers face a similar dilemma. A financial manager does not want to take too much risk because they want to be able to invest for the long-term to take advantage of the positive return bias of the financial markets. However, if they take too little risk even a positive result may not generate sufficient returns to meet the long-term goals of the strategy. So a financial manager must take sufficient risk to have a high probability of meeting their return target while minimizing the risk of a large drawdown in value which will be difficult to recover from. One way to do this is to diversify across many different risk factors. Owning a portfolio of a dozen different technology stocks is not enough as many technology stocks will be subject to the same risk factors and therefore may increase or decrease in unison in certain market environments. Similarly, a diversified bond portfolio may also be insufficient as most bonds decline in value when interest rates rise so all of the holdings may be exposed to the same interest rate risk factor. A truly diversified portfolio should include investments that are exposed to a variety of different risk factors such as interest rates, economic recession, inflation, market volatility, currency fluctuations, commodity prices, industry specific factors, etc. This way, should one risk factor result in big losses in a given area of the financial markets the loss as a percentage of the investor's total portfolio may be limited.

Perhaps one of the most common areas where individuals do not sufficiently manage their risk of financial ruin is excessive investment in employer stock. When an individual depends on the performance of their company for their employment income as well as their investment returns, they have a large percentage of their financial resources exposed to just one risk factor. Should the employer fall on hard times or experience an unexpected blow to their business the individual could face financial ruin as their income and investments could be adversely affected at the same time.

Another challenge could be a concentrated stock position. Often investors have stock holdings that have significantly appreciated in value and therefore would create a high tax liability if sold. However, if the stock price were to decline the resulting losses could have a major negative impact on the individual's overall net worth. In these cases, steps should be taken to mitigate the risk of financial ruin no matter how unlikely that may seem at the time. Even when an investor feels the odds are in their favor, they should still manage their risk by making sure they are only risking as much as they can afford to lose and still be able to continue on.

Real estate can also be an area where investors may have too much exposure to certain risk factors. Many individuals own a home and put a sizable portion of their investment assets into real estate as well. The problem is that even if the real estate holdings are diversified in terms of geography and property types (single family, multi-family, commercial, etc.) there are risk factors that they may have in common. For example, real estate values may be impacted by changes in interest rates, inflation, tax policy, lending standards, regulations, etc. In addition, real estate is often acquired by taking out a loan. Therefore, should prices decline the value of an investor's equity may decline at a higher rate causing a big decrease in wealth. It is even possible for prices to decline to the point where more is owned on a property than it is worth causing the value of the equity to turn negative.

The first step to mitigating the risk of financial ruin is for an individual to understand the risk factors that they are exposed to. This involves identifying the risks as well as the likelihood that they could result in a substantial financial loss. Too often people are unaware of the risks that they are taking which makes it impossible to take steps to reduce the impact that these risks may have on their finances. In addition, even when the risks are known many people are unable to accurately quantify the impact that the risk may have on their finances. This causes them to underestimate the size of the risks that they are taking.

The second step is to allocate financial resources among the different risks so that no one risk is likely to have too large of an impact on a financial plan. Individuals are often tempted to allocate a large portion of their financial resources to a hot investment, industry, or new technology. It may be prudent to favor a given opportunity if it is believed it will yield above average results. However, an investor should limit their exposure to a given risk factor, no matter how attractive it may appear, to an amount that will not derail the individual's financial plan should the opportunity not work out as expected. This is the part of financial planning that takes discipline, patience, and perspective. It can also be the difference between an individual having to rebuild their finances after a poor result versus dealing with an uncomfortable but manageable bump in the road.

Finally, the risk management plan should be adjusted as an individual's situation changes. When an individual's wealth increases their risk management plan may allow for greater risk as the loss of a given dollar amount will have a smaller impact than it would have had when their total wealth was much smaller. In addition, as an individual ages and their investment time horizon shortens, or they begin to take distributions to support their standard of living, their risk of financial ruin may increase. Therefore, the amount that they can expose to any given risk factor should be reviewed and monitored to protect against a major financial set back. Finally, there are times when a given risk factor may be risker than others. For example, when stock or real estate prices are high by historical standards the risk factors affecting those investments may be greater than during a more normal environment. When the economy is posed to enter recession the risk of a loss of employment income may be elevated. At these times the potential impact that these risk factors may have on the overall financial plan should be reassessed and the risk management plan should be updated to reflect the increased risk of financial ruin.

27

Contingency Planning

F inancial gains and losses can trigger responses in the emotional side of the brain. Financial gains can trigger the reward side of the brain creating a response similar to a sugar or caffeine high. Over time people can become addicted to this feeling. And like many other substances people often require larger and larger doses to get the same high so they take greater and greater risks in pursuit of large gains to produce the desired reward response in the brain. Losses can also trigger an emotional response such as the fight or flight response to external danger. This may include an increase of adrenalin in the body that makes the individual want to "do something" whether it be to abandon their long-term plan after a short-term setback or to increase their risk in an effort to quickly get back to even so that the bad feeling from the loss will subside. Unfortunately, these emotional responses can hinder financial decision making especially when the emotional side of the brain overrides the more rational and logical side of the brain which is more adept at weighing probabilities and planning for the future.

Everyone likes to think of themselves as composed and cool under pressure. However, the truth is that everyone is influenced to a greater or lesser degree by changes in their brain chemistry and the impulses that come with it. The key is to anticipate the emotional responses that will occur during periods of financial success and setbacks and create a plan to deal .with them ahead of time. No one can think entirely rationally when they are bombarded with positive or negative brain stimuli. So it is important to create guidelines that will dictate action ahead of time when the brain can rationally weigh the pros and cons of a given course of action rather than responding to external stimuli in the moment.

Creating a financial plan can be easy to do but difficult to follow. Plan assumptions that seem reasonable during times of financial stability may feel overly optimistic or pessimistic when volatility or uncertainty grips the economy and financial markets. This can cause an individual to question their plan and make changes during a time when their emotions have a greater influence on their decision making. This is not to say that a change in the economy or the markets may not warrant a response. The problem is that an emotional response may not be the best course of action to help an individual achieve their long-term goals. Instead, contingency plans should be put in place ahead of time, when the rational brain can weigh the costs and benefits, so that there is a rational plan of action in place when emotions run high.

Creating a contingency plan involves taking the time to question the assumptions of a financial plan ahead of time. Then create a plan of action that will be taken in response to a given change in the economic and financial landscape in order to keep the financial plan on track. By anticipating the potential challenges that an individual may face, the responses to those challenges can be formulated when they are able to think rationally about their long-term goals and objectives rather than succumbing to emotion. This will satisfy the need to "do something" when emotions run high but may increase the probability of doing the "right thing" by taking into account the long-term and short-term implications of a decision ahead of time rather than purely acting in response to recent events.

For example, what would be the impact and appropriate action if interest rates decrease so that bond prices rally but expected future returns are depressed? An emotional reaction may be to purchase more bonds due to their recent strong performance. A more rational plan of action may be to use the gains in bonds to pay off higher interest debt, such as a mortgage, that was taken out when interest rates were higher, or refinance the mortgage to lower the interest costs so that it is more in-line with the lower expected return on the bond portfolio. Reacting only to the positive stimuli (increased bond prices) could cause one to overlook the risk (lower interest rates that lead to lower potential long-term returns on bonds). While the positive short-term implications of higher bonds prices may be nice, a contingency plan may call for taking profits by selling bonds or implementing a strategy that takes advantage of the lower interest rate environment.

Managing stock market risk can also be an important use of contingency planning. Studies show that too many people have a tendency to increase their risk when stock prices are high and then sell their investments after prices drop and the losses become too emotionally uncomfortable. This pattern is the result of emotional reactions rather than a rational approach to investing.

Another option is to create a contingency plan that maintains diversification (holding assets that are exposed to different risk factors) through the periodic rebalancing of a portfolio when there is a large swing in prices. Many rebalancing programs (selling assets that have increased in value at an above average rate, and therefore exceed the target percentage of the overall investment mix, and buying assets that have not performed as well and as a result are below their target allocation) force investors to sell investments that have increased in value while buying investments that have decreased in value. This can maintain the overall risk profile while avoiding the urge to increase the allocation to hot investments or dump investments that have declined in value, and as a result, are selling at unattractive prices.

Using a trend-following approach to increase or decrease investment risk when there is a change in price trends can also be a part of a contingency plan. Rather than waiting until emotions dictate investment decisions it can be useful to anticipate those emotions and act in a proactive manner to adjust investment risk when market trends appear to change. This strategy may not always be successful, but it may minimize the damage by using a rational, rules-based strategy rather than one driven by emotion.

Finally, creating an allocation plan that includes low-risk investments to meet income needs during a period of poor market returns can help to sooth an investor's emotions. If an investor knows that they have several years' worth of income invested in low risk investments that can easily be sold to meet income needs it may reduce their anxiety level during periods of market volatility.

A contingency plan can also be put in place to address the unexpected loss of household income due to job loss or investment losses. One way to do this is to create a household budget that is based on the expected income available in a poor job market or when the financial markets are performing poorly (see The Next Best Alternative). Another option is to resist amassing high debt levels which can make it more difficult to adapt when household income declines. Finally, it is advisable to have an emergency fund that can cover at least several months of living expenses should there be an interruption in income. The financial security from an emergency fund can make the loss of income feel less scary and therefore help to reduce the likelihood of a negative emotional reaction.

Having a plan of action before emotions try to take control of financial decisions can decrease the likelihood of making a major financial mistake. This requires having a plan to address any changes in financial assumptions while maintaining a focus on achieving long-term financial goals. In other words, it is important to plan a primary course as well as alternate courses of action that can be taken should things not work out as planned rather than plotting an entirely new course during an emotionally charged time.

28

Risk Variation

Knowing when to change investment risk can be a tricky proposition. Naturally it may be prudent to reduce risk over time as an investor nears retirement or an age when they will need to pull income from their investments. In addition, a change in an investor's financial circumstances may prompt a need to review their risk level. However, the short-term timing of when and how to reduce risk is always a challenge. When the financial markets are doing well investors rarely want to reduce risk as they are enjoying the increased profits that their higher risk level is generating. Why not stick with a winning strategy? When investment markets are down many investors do not want to reduce risk because they become fixated on recovering their losses. Investors who frame their investment decisions based on the decline from a previous high point will often have a tendency to focus on getting back to even regardless of their financial circumstances or the market conditions. This desire to get back to even may cause an investor to hold on to risky assets for too long or to increase their risk in an effort to recover their losses quickly.

When things go poorly there can be a natural tendency to double down on the belief that things will turn around. For example, a blackjack player who loses several hands in a row may double their bet in an attempt to recover their losses. Casinos count on these betting strategies because they know the outcome of the previous hands have little impact on the outcome of the next hand. Therefore, the increased bet only accelerates the pace at which the casino is likely to get the gambler's money and free up a seat for the next victim. The irony is that this tendency is actually the opposite of the optimal strategy.

Instead of increasing risk in an effort to get back to even, or to a previous high point, the optimal strategy is to reduce risk following losses. This is based on a concept called the Kelly Criterion developed by J. L. Kelly, Jr. in 1956. The idea is that an individual should vary their risk in a way to avoid ruin. In this case, an investor that loses money should actually reduce their risk to reduce the likelihood of similar future losses. This way, should losses persist the investor will take less and less risk in order to preserve capital and limit the risk that the losses will eventually be so great that the investor will sell out completely or will not be able to fund their income needs.

The opposite is also true. When an investor realizes positive results and their wealth grows, the optimal strategy (assuming they do not spend the gains and their objective is to maximize their wealth rather than financial stability) is to increase their risk level. From a financial perspective this makes sense. All else equal, as an investor's wealth increases their ability to take risk increases as well (see Three Aspects of Risk) because they can afford to suffer greater losses without putting their ability to fund their basic needs in jeopardy.

One way to implement this strategy is to use a Constant Proportion Portfolio Insurance rebalancing strategy. To use this strategy an investor must determine a "portfolio floor" which is the value that could be invested in low risk assets and still meet the investor's income needs. The investor would then subtract the portfolio floor from the total value of their investment assets. Twice the resulting amount would then be invested in risky assets with the remainder invested in low risk assets. For example, if an investor has total investment assets of $500,000 and the portfolio floor is $300,000 then $400,000 ($500,000 value - $300,000 floor = $200,000 x 2 = $400,000) is invested in risky assets and $100,000 would be invested in low risk assets (80% risk assets). Should the value of the investments fall to $400,000 the amount invested in risky assets will decline to $200,000 ($400,000 value - $300,000 floor = $100,000 x 2 = $200,000) with the remaining $200,000 invested in low risk assets. So, when the value of the total portfolio decreased by 20% from $500,000 to $400,000 the proportion invested in risk assets declined from 80% of the portfolio to 50% to protect against further losses. On the other hand, should the value of the investment increase to $600,000 the amount invested in risky assets would increase to $600,000 ($600,000 value - $300,000 floor = $300,000 x 2 = $600,000) with nothing invested in low risk assets. In this case, a 20% increase in the portfolio value from $500,000 to $600,000 will cause the allocation to risky assets to increase from 80% to 100% as the investor can afford to take more risk given that they have $600,000, or double the amount of money needed ($300,000) to fund their income needs.

Obviously, an investor using such a strategy would still need to use risk management tools to manage the risk of loss on the portion of the portfolio invested in risky assets. In addition, such a strategy would require constant monitoring and regular rebalancing so that the risk level is reduced quickly should investment losses occur. Lastly, investors must be able to fight their emotions which may lead them to want to do the opposite of what they should do.

Naturally, such a strategy may not be suitable for most investors as it may be reasonable in theory but difficult to implement in practice. Investors who cannot handle the emotional toll of such a strategy should not engage in a variable risk strategy because they are more likely to subtract value rather than add value to their investment results.

29

Losses vs. Missed Profits

Financial capital (savings, investments, home equity, etc.) is a scarce resource. Most people have limited earning potential over their lifetime and are unlikely to receive a major financial windfall in the form of a sizable inheritance, lottery winnings, or large stock option payout. Therefore, a major financial setback due to investment losses or a decline in home value can be difficult to recover from, especially if the loss persists for many years or decades. In fact, statistics have shown that many households have yet to recover from the Great Recession a decade after it officially ended highlighting the damages that major financial losses can do to a household's financial well-being.

Financial risk and expected return are linked so that investors must be willing to accept some risk if they hope to realize a rate of return that exceeds the rate of inflation after income taxes are factored in. However, risk management strategies such as asset allocation, diversification, and rebalancing can be used to manage the risk of loss and reduce the likelihood that any losses will persist over a long period. Large losses, especially permanent losses, should be avoided as much as possible.

Unfortunately, many people have a difficult time distinguishing between losses and the missed opportunity for profits. Often an actual loss and a lost opportunity can feel the same as both trigger the same emotion of regret. One is the regret of taking too much risk resulting in losses and reduced wealth. The other is regret over not taking enough risk and missing out on profits resulting in wealth that is less than it could have been. However, while the emotional reaction may often be the same, the financial impact of a lost opportunity is fairly small whereas the impact of an actual financial loss can be quite large. The problem is too many people make financial decisions based on a fear of missing out rather than an objective assessment of their financial needs. It can also cause an individual to take too much risk, especially when past returns have been good. This can cause the fear of missing out (the fear of missed profits) to lead to actual losses and real financial challenges.

The key difference between an actual loss and a missed opportunity to profit is that actual losses leave an individual with depleted financial capital which not only has a negative impact on their current financial situation but also reduces their future earning potential because there is less capital to invest in future opportunities. A missed profit opportunity does not reduce an individual's future earning potential. In addition, opportunities to profit are not limited to just a few during a person's lifetime, they are constantly presenting themselves in many different forms over all stages of the economic and market cycles. If an individual misses out on a profit opportunity they can work on identifying the next opportunity without any real damage being done. This strategy may be superior to chasing lost opportunities by buying into investment fads or too-good-to-be-true investment schemes.

For example, the technology, media, and telecom boom of the late 1990s may have been caused by a fear-of-missing-out as many investors piled into technology stocks that were backed by little more than a website and a business plan. Many of these investors suffered a large decrease in their financial resources when previously high-flying technology companies went bankrupt. Yet investors who stayed disciplined and diversified were able to take advantage of the strong returns in real estate and commodities that occurred when the value of many technology stocks crashed or even went to zero. Similarly, investors who bid up real estate values in 2006 and 2007, chasing the above average returns of the early 2000s, may have missed the return available in long-term US Treasury bonds and gold that followed the sharp decline in real estate values.

Naturally, perpetually missing out on investment opportunities will make it difficult to achieve the rate of return required to achieve long-term financial goals. An excessive fear of risk and financial losses can lead to investment paralysis and low returns. For most it is important to take some financial risks but those risks should be measured against the need to take risk and should be influenced more by a fear of losses than a fear of missing out.

30

Consolidate Gains

Making money can create a strong emotional reaction. Think of how people react when they get on a hot streak at a craps table in a casino. Often the cheers can be heard throughout the gaming floor as the gamblers high-five or hug the complete strangers crowded next to them at the table. They are riding a high that is triggered by winning. Unfortunately, many of them will continue to chase that high well after the dice go cold and will eventually give back their winnings along with their hard-earned seed money that they brought to the table. Too often this pattern plays out the same way in personal finance. People chase the rush that comes with a large financial windfall rather than periodically consolidating their gains to build a more secure financial foundation.

Making money can actually change an individual's brain chemistry. The body releases dopamine which is a chemical that affects human emotions, specifically reward-motivated behaviors. This is what triggers the high or the rush that comes with making money. Dopamine is also associated with addictive activities such as drug use, playing video games, or gambling which also can trigger a surge in dopamine in the brain. Unfortunately, this can encourage people to engage in self-destructive behavior. In addition, people often need to increase the stakes to get the same dopamine high. For example, a gambler who wins $50 may feel a dopamine rush. But the next time they win $50 it may not feel as pleasurable. So, they increase their bet to win $100 to get the same rush as winning $50 triggered before. However, $100 soon will not do the trick causing them to perpetually up the stakes until a losing streak wipes them out. In this way dopamine can cause people to make poor financial decisions with dire consequences for their long-term financial security.

In finance, dopamine often causes people to take excessive risk. After experiencing gains investors may increase their allocation to the investments that performed the best or may seek out higher risk investments in an attempt to increase their potential gains. For example, during the real estate boom from 2002-2008 many real estate investors cashed out some of the equity in their existing properties to acquire more real estate holdings. When the real estate market finally crashed the value of their holdings plummeted. In some cases, the values decreased to the point where they were worth less than was owed.

In other cases, investors may continue to hold risky assets after they have increased in value to the point where they represent a large percentage of their net worth. For example, many people who became multi-millionaires during the tech boom of the late 1990s continued to hold their company stock options rather than reducing their risk or diversifying their investments. Many of them lost substantial investment value when tech stocks crashed in the early 2000s. Basically, wealthy people chased even greater wealth (and the next dopamine hit) and ended up with little investment value in the end.

Finally, some investors may seek out investments that offer a low probability of very high returns and a high probability of total loss (a return profile that mimics casino games). For example, investing in stocks issued by very small companies, stocks backed by distressed companies that are on the verge of bankruptcy, or stock options. When these investments go up in value, they may generate large gains, producing a jolt of dopamine, but they often become worthless making them poor investments on average.

The negative impacts of these behaviors can be financially and psychologically devastating. The utility function (discussed previously in Chapter 13) shows how financial losses are psychologically more painful than gains of an equal amount. Chasing gains can often lead to large losses which can result in real financial hardship and even depression. Psychologically, large losses can also make it difficult to rebuild wealth. It can be challenging to find the motivation to work and save for years or even decades to make up for past losses. Losses can also create an urge to get back to even quickly. This can lead to erratic behavior rather than the implementation of a reasonable financial plan.

So how does someone protect themselves from making these mistakes? The answer is to resist the urge to chase the next dopamine high by periodically consolidating gains. This can take several forms. One is to diversify investments that grow to become too large in proportion to net worth. This may mean selling concentrated stock positions to diversify into other stocks or buy lower risk investments. Rebalancing (selling assets or asset classes that have increased in value to buy assets or asset classes that have not performed as well) can also be a disciplined way to maintain a specific risk target rather than allowing the risk level to increase over time. It can also be beneficial to maintain an investment strategy that is grounded in solid economic and financial principles. This may make it easier to avoid chasing hot tips, too-good-to-be-true investment schemes, or investments with high risk and a low probability of success.

Consolidating gains does not mean avoiding risk altogether. Rather it involves shifting a portion of the gains that are made into safer options so that they are likely to be retained over the long-term. This means slowly building a financial foundation that may retain its value through good times and bad. The larger and more stable the financial foundation the more an investor can afford to take risk with their remaining assets while staying on track to achieve financial security.

31

Interest Rates and Bond Returns

Bond investing is often synonymous with low risk and low returns. In general, this can be true when dealing with highly rated, low yielding, short-term bonds. This is because in the long-run the primary source of return for highly rated bonds tends to be the periodic interest payments. However, during periods of high interest rate volatility bond prices can fluctuate wildly. In general, when interest rates rise bond prices fall and when interest rates fall bond prices rise. Therefore, when interest rates fall bond investors often get excited as their total return (interest payments plus price appreciation) can be larger than expected. In contrast, when interest rates rise it can leave bond investors disappointed as the decline in the value of their bonds may offset some, or all, of the interest received and can even lead to a negative total return in a given year. However, if one takes a long-term view an increase in interest rates may be viewed positively despite generating poor short-term returns and a decline in interest rates may be viewed negatively despite generating good short-term returns.

The difference between a short-term experience and long-term outlook comes down to reinvestment rates. Reinvestment rates are the interest rates that bond investors are able to get when they reinvest the interest and principle payments from the bonds that they own. When interest rates fall, bond prices rise but the interest paid on comparable bonds available in the market, as well as newly issued bonds, will be lower. Therefore, when a bond pays interest or principal payments those cash flows must be reinvested at the new lower interest rate unless the investor increases their risk level. In this case, the attractive short-term returns from falling interest rates may lead to lower returns over the longer-term. In a way, the higher returns on bonds due to falling interest rates is like borrowing on the future with interest. The long-term cost in the form of lower future interest payments can greatly outweigh the short-term benefit of higher bond prices.

On the other hand, rising interest rates can lead to lower bond returns in the short-term but may offer an opportunity to invest future cash flows at a higher interest rate, which may lead to greater returns over the long-term. In a way, suffering the poor short-term returns in exchange for the potential for greater long-term returns is a form of delayed gratification. Investors sacrifice some of their investment value in exchange for higher expected interest payments out into the future. Of course, the higher potential long-term returns can only be realized by those who maintain a disciplined long-term approach to bond investing. Those who sell after short-term losses will fail to capture any long-term opportunity.

It is also important that bond investors maintain a disciplined approach to risk management through periods of rising and falling interest rates. Often when interest rates and prospective future bond returns decline investors increase their risk level by investing in bonds with lower credit ratings. However, lower rated bonds carry a higher risk of default (risk the bond interest or principle will not be paid as agreed) which may put the investor's principal at greater risk than the short-term losses that may result from an increase in interest rates. Interest rates often decline during periods of economic weakness. A weak economy may make it more challenging for lower-rated bond issuers to generate the revenue needed to make the interest and principle payments on their bonds. Therefore, it is important for investors to maintain a disciplined risk management approach when the economy falters and interest rates decline rather than chase bonds paying higher interest rates.

When interest rates rise many investors abandon bonds due to poor short-term returns. Bonds are often a source of stability in a balanced stock and bond portfolio and thus represent a key risk management tool. Therefore, moving out of bonds may be akin to increasing the risk of an investment portfolio beyond what is otherwise reasonable given an investor's financial goals.

Of course, there are some strategies that investors can use to manage the risk of rising interest rates. For example, mortgage-backed bonds pay interest and principal every month whereas traditional bonds only make interest payments every six months and pay the principal as a lump-sum at the end of the term. In a rising interest rate environment, the accelerated cash flow from mortgage bonds can then be reinvested at higher interest rates. When interest rates are rising this will increase the overall yield of the bond portfolio at a faster pace than it would if the portfolio were invested in bonds with a more traditional payment schedule.

Another strategy is a bond ladder. This involves purchasing bonds that will mature every six months or every year. For example, a portfolio may be invested in bonds with a one-year, two-year, three-year, four-year, and five-year maturity so that one of the bonds will mature every year for the next five years. When a bond matures it can be reinvested with a maturity one year longer than the longest bond in the ladder. The result is a large cash flow every year when a bond matures which can be reinvested at higher interest rates should interest rates continue to rise. In addition, the principal that is reinvested each year is used to purchase longer-term bonds which typically pay higher interest rates than shorter-term bonds while the average term of the portfolio remains fairly constant.

Investors don't need to fear rising interest rates as there are strategies that can be implemented to manage interest rate risk. However, even if an increase in interest rates catches an investor by surprise leading to poor short-term returns the resulting increase in potential future returns may more than compensate for the loses over the longer-term. The key is to maintain a disciplined risk management approach focused on long-term results rather than focusing on short-term fluctuations in bond prices.

32

Borrowing on Future Growth

Borrowing on the future is a dominate characteristic of modern society. A large portion of the economy is dependent on the access to credit that allows consumers to buy now and pay later. However, this dynamic is also a major contributing factor to the boom and bust nature of the business cycle (economic growth cycle). When a consumer borrows on their future earnings to make a purchase today, they are pulling what would otherwise be future expenditures into the present time period. This stimulates current economic growth which is highly dependent on consumer spending. As long as incomes increase over time it may be able to support increased spending and higher debt payments. However, if incomes stagnate or grow too slowly, borrowing on the future may have a dampening effect on future economic growth as there may be less income available to fund future purchases. Consumers may then be forced to cut back on spending as their income will already be committed to making debt payments to pay for past purchases. When consumers are forced to cut back it can cause the rate of economic growth to slow or even trigger a recession (period of negative economic growth). In a recession, incomes may decline further causing an even greater pullback in consumer spending as debt payments make up a larger and larger percentage of household income and therefore spending must be cut even further. Eventually this can lead to loan defaults, charge-offs, or even bankruptcies which may wipe out a portion of the debt burden. With the amount of debt reduced the cycle may start over as consumers once again increase spending by borrowing on future earnings. So, a period of strong consumer spending that drives economic growth can lead to weaker spending and slower economic growth in the future. This is called the debt cycle and can be a major contributor to the boom and bust cycle of economic activity (see Debt Cycle).

A similar pattern can be observed in the boom and bust pattern of the stock market. When the stock market has a good year many investors get excited. This is especially the case when the market has a string of several good years in a row. The excitement can lead to euphoria and draw in more and more investors who want to participate in the gains. In addition, existing investors often increase the risk of their investments in an attempt to capture larger returns. The problem is that when stock market returns are above average investors may be borrowing on future returns without realizing it. When short-term investment returns exceed those that can be justified by the fundamental factors that drive the stock market over the long-term then future returns are more likely to be below average or negative when the stock market finally corrects. So strong returns may be exciting in the short-term but can lead to disappointment in the longer-term.

The key is to be able to assess when market returns are justified and when they are not. This question can come down to a few key factors that drive the long-term value of the stock market. These factors can be used to estimate the average annual returns for the market as well as estimate future returns when past returns have deviated from that average.

It all starts with corporate earnings. After all, the primary reason that an individual would invest in a company is to participate in the earnings that it generates. While corporate earnings fluctuate with the different stages of the economic cycle their growth rate can be quite consistent over the long-term averaging 5-6% per year. This is because corporate earnings are influenced by the rate of global economic growth. It follows that corporations cannot grow their earnings at a rate that far exceeds the overall rate of economic growth. Given that global economic growth is constrained by factors that increase fairly slowly and steadily over time; namely land, labor, investment capital, and technological innovation; the natural rate of corporate earnings growth is also likely to be constrained by these factors. A distinction is made between the natural rate and the actual rate of growth because at times corporate earnings growth may fall below the natural rate of growth due to resource constraints. At other times it may surge ahead as companies pull future sales into the present by offering sales incentives or when customers buy on credit using future earnings to buy goods and services today. However, over the longer-term the rate of growth will typically revert to the long-term average.

The second source of return is the dividends companies pay out to their shareholders. Typically, companies increase their dividends slowly over time as their earnings increase. Most companies want to avoid cutting their dividends because it sends the wrong message to investors who may depend on the dividend for regular income. For this reason, they often only raise their dividend when they are confident that the earnings that will be paid out as a dividend are sustainable. Therefore, when stock prices rise quickly dividends typically do not keep pace so that the dividend yield (dividend per share as a percentage of the stock price) declines. In contrast, when stock prices are low the dividend yield will often be higher. This is important because over time dividends, especially if they are reinvested, are an important source of return from investing in stocks.

So, if stock prices are determined by long-term earnings growth and dividends, both of which tend to grow at a steady rate over the long-term, why are stock prices so volatile? It comes down to the third source of return which is the earnings multiple, most commonly referred to as the price-to-earnings (P/E) ratio. The P/E ratio is a stock's price per share divided by its earnings per share. Put another way it is the price investors are willing to pay for one dollar of earnings. When the P/E ratio is lower than average investors may be getting a bargain and when it is higher than average investors may be overpaying.

When stock prices increase at a faster pace than earnings the P/E ratio increases and when prices fail to keep up with earnings growth the P/E ratio declines. However, similar to earnings growth rates, the P/E ratio tends to revert to the mean (return to the average) over time. Therefore, a P/E ratio that is below the long-term average could be viewed as an opportunity and a P/E ratio that is above the long-term average should be viewed with caution.

Using this three-factor model one can estimate the long-term return for the stock market. Since 1950 the earnings per share for the S&P 500 stock index has increased at an average annual rate of 5.78% and the dividend yield averaged 2.82%. Had the P/E ratio remained stable at the median (half of the time it's higher and half the time its lower) of 16.9 the average annual return for the S&P 500 would have been 8.58%. Of course, the P/E ratio did not remain stable but rather increased producing a total return (price appreciation plus dividend yield) of 10.46% over that time period. However, should the P/E ratio revert back to the median of 16.9 in the future the average annual return would likely fall below the estimate of 8.58% in future years to average down the above average returns reported since 1950.

In late 2017 the P/E ratio of the S&P 500 index stood at 24.7 based on the trailing 12-month earnings of $107 and an index value of 2,648. Assuming future earnings were to grow at the long-term average of 5.78% over the following 10 years the earnings in the year 2027 would be $188. Assuming the P/E ratio reverts to its long-term median of 16.9 the value of the S&P 500 index would be 3,177 after a decade. This equates to an average annual return, excluding dividends, of just 1.84%, well below the long-term average earnings growth rate of 5.78%. When the 2017 dividend yield of 1.88% is added in, the estimated total return for the S&P 500 over the decade is just 3.72% (1.84% plus 1.88%) as opposed to the expected long-term average of 8.58% and the 10.46% return realized since 1950. In other words, the high returns of the market in recent years may have simply resulted from investors pulling future returns forward so that the pace of future returns will need to moderate to correct for past overpricing.

Of course, there are multiple paths that stock prices can take to achieve the estimated average annual return. One option is that prices increase at a slower rate than earnings to correct for the above average P/E ratio. Another option is that investors decide that the potential return from holding stocks is too low to compensate for the risk. In this case, investors may sell causing prices to decline sharply to the point where the P/E ratio reverts to its long-term median and potential future returns revert to the estimated long-term average. For example, holding S&P 500 earnings fixed at $107 and assuming the P/E ratio will revert to the long-term median of 16.9 equates to a 32% decrease in the value of the index.

This conundrum demonstrates how above average returns that exceed the pace of earnings growth plus the dividend yield may lead to poor future returns, including the possibility of a sharp decline in stock prices. It also demonstrates the cause and effect of the boom and bust cycle of the stock market that occurs when future returns are pulled into the present due to outsized market gains. This borrowing on the future, as with consumer borrowing, must be paid back at some point. Therefore, investors should pay close attention to these factors in order to estimate future market returns and manage their risk exposure through the different phases of stock market cycles.

33

The Chicken and the Hog

nvestment strategies have been compared to raising chickens and raising hogs. When raising hogs, the animals increase in value over time as they gain weight and the return is only realized at the end when the animal is sold at market. When raising chickens, a smaller periodic return is realized over time as the eggs are sold with no big payoff at the end. Some argue that one strategy is superior to the other but in reality both have their merits and both have times when they may be in or out of favor.

Raising chickens is similar to investing in high dividend paying stocks, bonds, or income producing real estate. The primary purpose is to collect the periodic payments with the hope that the yield will increase over time as companies increase their dividends, rents are increased, or bonds mature and are reinvested at higher interest rates. This strategy is used by many retirees who live off the income from their investments while leaving their principle intact. This can be a good strategy from a behavioral finance standpoint as it forces spending discipline by limiting the amount that can be spent to the amount of income that is generated each year. Assuming an investor starts with a large enough savings the income generated may be sufficient to maintain their standard of living for a lifetime.

Of course, this strategy can also have its drawbacks. If a company is forced to cut its dividend due to financial distress, real estate rents decline, or a bond matures and must be reinvested at a lower interest rate the income from the portfolio will decline. This may necessitate a reduction in spending. However, if the decrease is too great it may be unreasonable to decrease spending by enough to offset the reduction in income. In this case, investments may need to be sold to supplement spending. This is akin to a chicken farmer selling hens to supplement their income from selling eggs. The problem is that the next year fewer eggs will be produced possibly requiring the farmer to sell off more chickens. This trend may continue with a greater number of chickens sold each year until eventually the farm goes under. A similar thing can happen to an investor who must sell income producing investments to supplement income. The level of income will decline over time requiring larger and larger sales until the portfolio is exhausted. This can be especially problematic when investing in assets like real estate because the sale of such a high value asset will reduce the income generated by a large amount.

Another problem is when income investing is in vogue investors may bid up the price of income producing assets so that the income produced is a small percentage of the investment value. For example, if too many people decided to get into the egg producing business the cost of hens could be bid up and the price of eggs may drop. Similarly, if too many people purchase income producing assets, such as bonds, they will bid up the price causing interest rates to decline. Under these circumstances income investing may be less attractive than other strategies.

In addition, income investors cannot stomach the volatility of some income investments, such as dividend paying stocks or real estate. While the strategy of buying and holding high dividend paying stocks may seem attractive when stock prices are trending upward it can be difficult to maintain when stock prices are plummeting. This can lead to a difficult decision. It's like a chicken farmer choosing what to do with sick hens. There are three primary outcomes. The hens could recover to health, the hens could die and become worthless, or the farmer could sell the hens at a deeply discounted price to that of healthy hens. An investor who owns stocks, bonds, or real estate that have sharply declined in value may face a similar dilemma. They can hold the investment and hope for a recovery; hold the investment until the company goes bankrupt, the bond defaults, or the real estate is foreclosed; or they can sell at a deeply discounted value. In this case, two of the three scenarios can lead to a poor investment outcome.

Finally, income producing assets tend to rise and fall in value in response to changes in the same risk factors which can lead to a lack of diversification. This can cause investors to take more risk than they realize due to a concentration of risk factors in their investment portfolio. For example, when interest rates rise it can cause the value of high dividend stocks, bonds, and income producing real estate to all decline in value. This is akin to a chicken farmer with a barn full of hens with little genetic diversity so that they are susceptible to the same diseases. Should things go bad there will be little value left in the barn just as the value of an investor's income portfolio may be greatly reduced should interest rate increase.

Hog farming, on the other hand, is similar to investing in growth stocks or commodities, such as gold, which do not pay income. This strategy is often used by individuals who are saving for long-term goals, such as retirement. Since these investors do not need periodic income they may favor investments with the potential to grow so that they can be sold in the future and the proceeds can be used to fund spending needs or reinvested into a different investment strategy. Since there is little, or no, income from these investments this strategy focuses primarily on price appreciation as the sole source of return. As long as the rate of appreciation is sufficient to result in the amount needed to fund long-term goals it may be a successful strategy.

One problem with the hog farming investment style is that it is largely dependent on the state of the market when it is time to sell. If too many hogs are brought to market in one year the price offered will likely be low no matter how many years were invested in fattening them up. Since there is no periodic income generated the entire return from the investment strategy is dependent on the price at the time of sale. This can be a risk for growth-oriented investors who may be faced with a weak stock or commodities market when they desire to change investment strategies or need to sell investments to fund their long-term goals.

Another problem is that declining asset prices often go hand-in-hand with economic contraction (recession). A poor economy may force an investor to sell investments to make up for lost income from other sources, such as wages. If this occurs when the investment markets are also poor, investors may have to sell assets at prices that trigger a loss or lock-in a below target rate of return. For a hog farmer this is similar to the challenge of a bad winter. Severe storms can necessitate making repairs to the farm which may require selling hogs that are sickly or below weight and therefore fetch a low price. A simultaneous deterioration of the overall climate and an individual's circumstances can lead to a big financial setback or even ruin.

In addition, the companies that are represented by stock investments, like hogs, have a life cycle. Companies begin in the start-up stage in which the company is formed and begins operations. If the company is successful it will enter the growth stage in which sales increase rapidly and the value of the company will likely increase. Eventually, after the opportunities for growth are captured and a company achieves sufficient size compared to the size of its market, or competitors move in to increase competition, the company will reach the maturity stage. In this stage sales growth slows as does the rate of stock price appreciation. Finally, should the company falter, or its markets be displaced by innovation, the company may enter the decline stage which can eventually lead to failure. This is similar to the cycle of a hog which starts out small and scrawny but can pack on the pounds quickly as it matures. Eventually the hog reaches a size where the rate of weight gain slows. Finally, if the hog lives long enough it will begin to lose weight as it enters old age. For a growth strategy to be successful it is important to identify the stage that an investment is in, although this is not easy. A decline in sales for a company or the loss of weight for a hog may be a sign of entering the decline stage or it may be a temporary issue that will be overcome. For this reason, such a strategy requires constant monitoring.

 Finally, when things go well a growth strategy can lead to outsized returns over a short time period which can attract speculators who bid prices up further. These periods are often referred to as bubbles which can be incredibly damaging when they burst. This has occurred many times in a variety of investment markets. It has also occurred many times in the livestock market. For example, during World War I and World War II cattle prices skyrocketed as European cattle production stopped and transportation from South America became too risky. This caused beef prices to surge enticing spectators to enter the cattle ranching business. Then after the war the demand for US beef fell. The decline in demand combined with the high supply caused beef prices to plummet driving many cattle ranchers out of business. Similar boom and bust stories have played out in the gold and oil markets, with technology and financial stocks, and the real estate market (see Cycles).

With risks associated with income investing and growth investing, chicken and hog farming, what should investors do? First, an investor must accept that risk is a part of investing. Second, an investor must do their best to manage their risk. One of the best ways to manage risk is diversification. Engaging in growth oriented and income-oriented investing (chicken farming and hog farming) simultaneously can be a way of benefiting from each strategy while mitigating the risk of implementing each strategy independently.

34

Real Assets vs. Paper Assets

arket cycles often have themes that define them. For example, the late 1970s market cycle was defined by high inflation and soaring commodity prices. In the 1980s the theme was leveraged buyouts fueled by the issuance of junk bonds. In the early 1990s there was a real estate boom that eventually led to the savings and loan crisis. In the late 1990s the internet emerged as a tool for communication and commerce and technology stocks led the way on Wall Street. This then gave way to the real estate and commodities boom that defined the period from 2001-2008 and sowed the seeds for the financial crisis that followed. Finally, the current period has been defined by low interest rates, stock buybacks (companies borrowing or using free cash flow to buyback their own shares), and over a decade of strong stock market returns.

Naturally, it would have been beneficial to have identified these themes beforehand as tremendous fortunes were made by these who got in on these themes early. Of course, fortunes were also lost by those who were late to the party. So, it is important to not only identify the theme early but also to have a sense of when it may have run its course and a period of transition (often accompanied by a recession) may be near.

Unfortunately, it is nearly impossible to identify a specific theme ahead of time. It is only in retrospect that a market cycle is defined by its excesses and eventual correction. However, taking a broad view there does appear to be a pattern that emerges: the transition from a market that favors real assets to one that favors paper assets in alternate succession.

Real assets are assets that are physical in nature, such as real estate, commodities, and investments in physical infrastructure. Paper assets are assets that are primarily a claim on intangible items such as intellectual property (copywrites, patents, and trademarks), debt obligations outlined in loan agreements, business plans for start-up companies, and other non-physical assets on company financial statements.

An examination of the market themes listed previously shows how real assets may be in favor for a time, then give way to paper assets, which eventually leads to real assets returning to prominence, and so on. In the late 1970s real assets were the dominate theme. Commodities, such as oil and gold, soared in price leading to major investments in the physical infrastructure required to extract them. High inflation pushed up the value of real estate and investors flocked to limited partnership investments that focused on constructing or acquiring physical assets.

In the 1980s the focus shifted to paper assets. Leverage buyouts funded by junk bonds (bond issued by companies with poor credit ratings that are backed by little or no physical collateral) were the way to get rich. This period is perhaps best personified by Michael Douglas' character Gordon Gekko in the movie *Wall Street*. In the movie Gekko makes his money through the hostile takeover of companies which are then reorganized or broken up and sold off at a profit. It is an example of money being made through financial engineering (activities designed to increase the value of an investment) not through the investment in real assets.

In the late 1980s and early 1990s real assets were in vogue again. There was investment in physical manufacturing capabilities, especially in Japan and emerging Asian countries, called Asian Tigers, at the time. Real estate values also soared fueled by a decline in interest rates and loose lending standards from savings and loans, many of which later failed. This theme continued until the recession and the collapse of the Japanese stock and real estate markets.

The mid and late 1990s was defined by the emergence of the internet and a shift in focus by investors from real assets to paper assets. Many of the technology company stocks that sold at high prices were backed by little more than a business plan and a website. A number of companies went public with very little in physical assets and no earnings, yet their stock prices surged. After the correction many investors were left with nothing more than paper, in the form of a stock certificate, to show for their investment.

Following the technology bubble the focus turned back to physical assets. Despite relatively benign inflation real estate prices surged increasing as much as 20% per year in some areas. In response, housing construction activity increased sharply as investors financed new projects. In addition, commodities, such as oil, became popular investments with oil prices peaking at over $150 per barrel. Even the debt instruments, such as mortgage-backed bonds, that dominated the bond market for years before leading to the downturn were backed by physical assets in the form of real estate collateral.

Finally, this brings us to the current market cycle in which paper assets are back in favor. Capital expenditures (business investment in real assets) have been persistently low. Instead businesses have taken advantage of low interest rates and used their free cash flow to buy back their own stock, another form of financial engineering. The increased demand is pushing up stock prices, but the gains are all on paper with the increase in value only appearing on company financial statements and investor account statements. Companies that are investing are primarily focused on intellectual property and mergers and acquisitions with "brick and mortar" businesses like traditional retailers, banks, and manufacturers losing out to companies with business plans that are reliant on less tangible assets.

So, the obvious next question is: How long will the current market cycle last and when will the focus shift from paper assets to real assets? This question is too difficult to answer with any certainty, but investors may benefit from being aware of this pattern and being on the lookout for signs that paper assets are falling out of favor. In addition, during the next market cycle it may be advantageous to put special emphasis on real assets when allocating investment capital.

35

Price to Rents Ratio

Threhe residential real estate market has recovered nicely from the doldrums of the Great Recession. This seems to have led to two diametrically opposed views on the market. Some have reverted back to the "fear of missing out" mentality that was prevalent during the 2005-2006 boom years. The fear is that prices will rise further and price them out of the market so they have to get in now or they will miss out. So they jump right in without looking before they leap. Others have taken the "here we go again" mentality. They assume that rising prices must mean a new bubble has formed and mayhem will soon follow. They often base this view on one data point: the trailing percentage increase in home prices. What is peculiar is that few people fall in the middle of these views. After all, if markets are efficient shouldn't prices be at or near fair value most of the time? So how can one test the market efficiency to develop an informed opinion about the residential real estate market?

One way to estimate the fair value (the value based on the facts and circumstances, not the current price) of residential real estate is to take a page from the stock analysts' playbook. Stock analysts often reference a company's price-to-earnings (P/E) ratio, a number that is derived by dividing a company's stock price per share by its earnings per share. Historically, the P/E ratio of the US stock market has averaged around 17. When the P/E ratio is 10 or less, stocks may be considered a bargain. After all, at those times investors are paying $10 for a dollar of earnings which normally sells for $17. On the other hand, when the P/E ratio is 20 or greater stocks may be considered to be expensive which could lead to below average returns in the future. Of course, the P/E ratio for individual companies may vary from the average due to a variety of factors including the expected earnings growth rate, interest rates, and the value of the company's assets and projected cash flows. Therefore, it is often instructive to compare an individual stock's current P/E ratio to its historical average and the P/E ratio of its peers to assess whether the stock may be a bargain or overpriced.

A similar strategy can be used to value residential real estate, but with real estate rents are used in place of earnings. After all, rental rates are the best approximation of the value of the shelter that residential real estate provides. A renter does not participate in the appreciation of the home so their rental rates will not reflect the speculative value that may be assigned to real estate when prices are trending upward. Renters also do not get tax breaks for renting real estate so tax policy will not impact the amount of rent they are willing to pay. Instead, rental rates are determined by the supply and demand for shelter. The supply of residential real estate is determined by the number of new homes built compared to those that are condemned. The demand for shelter is largely determined by population growth rates and the pace of new household formation. Both factors tend to change fairly slowly. Therefore, rental rates tend to be a fairly steady reflection of the fair value of residential real estate.

In contrast, at times real estate prices can fluctuate greatly. When the economy is doing well some choose to invest their increased income in homeownership, bidding up prices in the process. Naturally, some will financially over-extend themselves either by purchasing a home they cannot reasonably afford or by overly relying on the stability of their future income. When a recession eventually comes, and incomes decline, there will be some forced sellers which will drive prices down. In addition, investors and speculators, often enticed by upward trending prices, may buy homes causing prices to rise further. Then when the housing market stagnates or turns downward they may sell to cash-in on their investments causing prices to fall more than the long-term supply and demand equilibrium might dictate. The result is real estate prices that fluctuate to a greater degree than the fair value of shelter.

When real estate prices exceed their fair values prices often correct either by trending sideways while rental rates increase over time or prices decline to restore equilibrium. Often prices over-correct, a result of the psychological nature of markets, causing prices to fall below the fair value. Eventually, enough brave souls step in to buy and the recovery begins. So how can one gauge which stage the real estate market is in before buying or selling?

Similar to the Price-to-Earnings (P/E) ratio used to value stocks, the price-to-rents (P/R) ratio can be used to gauge the value of the real estate market. The price of residential real estate tends to average 15 times the annual rental rate. So a home that rents for $1,500 per month, or $18,000 per year, would have an average value of $270,000 ($18,000 times 15). If the home is selling for more the real estate market may be ahead of itself and if it is selling for less there may be a bargain to be had.

Knowing the state of the overall market can be useful when making a decision to buy or sell real estate. But all markets are local so it's just a jumping-off point. Just like stocks, some local markets may trade at a higher or lower price-to-rents ratio due to a variety of factors including past price appreciation, rent control laws, the availability of land to build, and demographics. Therefore, some real estate markets may exhibit a price-to-rents ratio that is consistently above or below 15, just as some stocks may consistently trade at a price-to-earnings ratio above or below the average. Individual market research is needed. It can be useful to determine the average long-term price-to-rents ratio for a local market or even a neighborhood when assessing a specific home. The price-to-rents ratio for a specific home compared to a longer-term average can be instructive as to the home's prospects as an investment.

Like the price-to-earnings ratio, the price-to-rents ratio is most useful at extremes. A price-to-rents ratio that is slightly above or below the long-term average is relatively meaningless. But when the price-to-rents ratio is well above the long-term average it may be a sign that the home is overpriced and therefore the long-term rate of appreciation may be below average. Conversely, when the price-to-rents ratio is well below the long-term average the future rate of appreciation may be attractive.

36

A Home is Not an Investment

For many people their home is the most valuable asset they own. This often means the value of their home equity makes up a large percentage of their total wealth and changes in the value of their home can cause their wealth to increase or decrease sharply. For this reason, many people often talk about "investing" in their home by making improvements such as upgrading, remodeling, and/or expanding their home. The problem is that personal use assets, such as a home, are no substitute for investment assets when it comes to planning for one's financial future.

One problem with investing in personal use assets is that they are used up over time. An expensive kitchen remodel may make a home look updated and allow it to sell at a premium price for a few years. But 10 years later the kitchen will once again start to look dated and any price premium will have disappeared. Other improvements have a limited life as well. Appliances, pools, HVAC systems, roofs, flooring, and landscaping are all used up over time so that they must eventually be replaced. The "investment" in the home is realized over time in the form of personal satisfaction from its use and enjoyment. Rarely do such "investments" result in a financial gain that can be used to achieve other financial goals such as funding retirement or a child's college education. Meanwhile, most traditional investment assets increase in value over time rather than decrease in value due to wear and tear, obsolescence, or changing style preferences.

Another problem with viewing a personal use asset, such as a home, as an investment is that the owner's standard of living increases as the asset appreciates. If someone purchases a home for $300,000 their standard of living will include a home valued at $300,000. Should the house increase in value to $500,000 their standard of living would then require $500,000 to be dedicated to housing even though they continue to live in the same home. So in reality the $200,000 increase in wealth is accompanied by a $200,000 increase in their standard of living. The only way the increase in value can be used to fund other financial goals is if the home is sold and the owner downgrades their living situation by living in a smaller home, moving to a less desirable area, or renting. Each of these options has drawbacks which may be realized to a greater or lesser extent depending on the individual's situation. In contrast, investment assets such as stocks and bonds can be liquidated to fund long-term financial goals without a direct negative impact to the owner's standard of living.

In addition, personal use assets often come with increased costs. Increasing the value of a home can come with increased property taxes and insurance costs, not to mention higher maintenance costs. This may reduce the money that can be saved or invested in other types of assets. In contrast, investment assets often produce income in the form of interest, dividends, rents, etc. that exceed any expenses and can be reinvested to acquire additional investment assets. The compounding of investment income can be a major source of financial wealth which may be needed to fund long-term financial goals.

Lastly, "investing" in a home often results in a very concentrated investment portfolio in which one property represents a large portion of total wealth. If the neighborhood or community in which the home is located falls on difficult times the value of real estate in that area may decrease. Should national or global factors have a negative impact on real estate values the value of the home may decline sharply. Local land use or tax policy could also make the home less desirable. Municipal infrastructure problems can lead to higher costs and a lower quality of life. Basically, there is a litany of issues that could impact a given home's value and make it a poor investment. On the other hand, purchasing traditional investments can make it much easier to diversify across many different types of assets that are exposed to a variety of different risk factors. This makes it less likely that all of the investments will increase or decrease in value at the same time leading to a reduced overall risk profile.

Given these factors, "investing" in a home is often a poor way to plan to fund long-term financial goals. Therefore, the investment in a home should be limited to the amount that an individual can afford to dedicate to personal use assets after their other long-term financial goals have been funded with more traditional investment assets.

37

Selling Liquidity Too Cheap

I n the investment world liquidity refers to how quickly an investment can be bought or sold without affecting the investment's price. When an investment is highly liquid an investor can buy or sell large dollar amounts of the investment quickly at a price close to the price quoted before the buy or sell order was placed. Liquidity largely depends on a large number of investors participating in the market for an investment. For example, the market for US government debt is highly liquid due to the large number of investors and institutions that hold government debt and participate in the market. On the other hand, the market for the stock of a small company may be illiquid as few investors may hold the stock and trading in the stock may be sporadic.

In financial planning, the term liquidity relates to how quickly and inexpensively an individual can get access to money that can be spent. Money that is deposited in a checking account would be considered highly liquid as the owner can write a check on the account at any time or withdrawal cash from an ATM. On the other hand, money deposited in a Certificate of Deposit (CD) would be considered less liquid because the money is locked up for the term of the CD or the owner must pay an early withdrawal penalty to get access to the money before the end of the term. CDs and other illiquid investments often pay the depositor a higher interest rate to compensate for the reduced liquidity. However, in many cases individuals give away or sell their liquidity far too cheaply rather than demanding a high enough rate of return to compensate for the reduced access to their money.

Liquidity is important because it represents an investment risk. Life is uncertain. Therefore, even when an individual does not expect to need access to their money there is a chance that their financial circumstances may change. For example, if an investor loses their job, a family member has an emergency and needs financial assistance, or a better investment opportunity becomes available the ability to access money may be quite valuable. For this reason, illiquidity represents a risk to an individual's overall financial plan. As with other risks, liquidity risk should either be avoided or individuals should demand a high enough rate of return to compensate for the risk. Yet too often liquidity risk is ignored.

One way that many individuals sell their liquidity too cheap is accepting investment lockup periods with little or no additional returns. This generally falls into two categories: Lack of marketability and costs to access money. Lack of marketability typically affects private (non-public) investments as well as some public investments that do not trade on an exchange. For example, many investments structured as limited partnerships and non-traded Real Estate Investment Trusts (REITs) are often very illiquid between their purchase date and payout date. That does not mean that these investments cannot be sold but there is often a long delay before the money can be accessed or the investment must be sold at a deep discount to its estimated value. Given the risk that this lack of liquidity presents one would expect investors to demand returns that greatly exceed those of other, more liquid investments. Yet in reality these illiquid investments often do not realize returns that exceed those of other options. So the lack of liquidity represents a risk that investors take with no additional return on their investment.

Investments that subject the owner to expenses to access their money are also considered illiquid due to the inability to access the full value of the investment quickly without discounting the value. These expenses are often labeled early redemption fees, surrender charges, or back-end loads. Whatever the name, these charges reduce the investment's liquidity and therefore increase the risk of loss or a poor return should the investor need to access their money due to a change in their financial circumstances. Yet many investment companies offer multiple classes of investments, some of which include charges to access the money for a given time period and some that do not. In this case an investor that accepts an investment with a lockup period, surrender period, or any other expense that restricts their access to their money is selling their liquidity and getting nothing in return.

A second way that individuals sell their liquidity too cheaply is to take out a mortgage with a shorter-term and higher minimum payment than other longer-term mortgage options. For example, some people will choose a 10 or 15-year mortgage rather than a 30-year mortgage because a shorter-term mortgage often comes with an interest rate that is 0.25% to 0.50% lower. However, a 15-year mortgage can have a payment that is one-and-a-half times that of a 30-year mortgage and a 10-year mortgage can have a minimum payment double that of a 30-year mortgage. So, while the borrower may save money in interest over the life of the loan they must commit a larger amount of their financial resources to mortgage payments or risk defaulting on the debt. Often the projected savings is quite small when compared to the lack of flexibility from the higher minimum payment. This is especially true when one factors in that a longer-term mortgage can generally be paid off faster without penalty. In other words, a borrower can take out a 30-year mortgage but make the larger payments of a 10 or 15-year mortgage to shorten the term. The term will still exceed 10 or 15 years by a few months due to the higher interest rate on the 30-year mortgage, but the borrower will have the flexibility to reduce the payment to the lower 30-year mortgage payment at any time. So, if the borrower loses their job or the retirement account they were counting on to provide income to pay the mortgage declines in value due to a market downturn they can reduce their monthly payment without defaulting on the debt. In many cases, this flexibility will be far more valuable than the expense of several months of additional mortgage payments.

A third way that illiquidity can create a problem is when an investor puts too much of their investable assets into illiquid investments like a small business or real estate. These investments can take time to sell and often can only be sold by paying high transaction costs in the form of commissions, listing fees, and/or attorney fees. In addition, they often can only be sold on an all-or-none basis. For example, if the owner of a rental home needs access to money they cannot sell only the garage, they must sell the entire home. In some cases, the owner may be able to borrow using the asset as collateral but this also comes with costs, limitations on the amount that can be borrowed, and potentially negative tax consequences if the asset is later sold. This does not mean that these investments should be avoided due to their lack of liquidity but rather that an investor should require a premium rate of return to accept the liquidity risk.

Private loans can be another investment where investors often sell their liquidity too cheaply. Private loans – a loan made by one individual to another – are often made at above market interest rates and in some cases can have tax benefits, such as when the loan is in conjunction with an installment sale. However, private loans are illiquid as they often cannot be sold and when they can it is often at a deep discount to the balance owed. Too often this lack of liquidity is overlooked on the assumption that the money lent will not be needed by the lender before the debt is paid. Therefore, the lender fails to charge an interest rate that will compensate them for the higher risk due to the illiquidity of the loan.

Finally, illiquid investments can create problems in retirement accounts. Many retirement accounts require that the account owner take distributions after reaching age 70.5. Since illiquid investments either cannot be sold or can only be sold at discounted values the entire amount often must be distributed leading to a greater tax liability than if just the minimum amount required by law were distributed. In this case, investors should not only demand a higher rate of return to compensate for the illiquidity of the investment but should also expect to earn a higher rate of return to offset the potential for a higher tax liability.

It should be stressed that illiquid investments and borrowing strategies do not need to be avoided outright. However, it is important that plans be in place to mitigate the risks that illiquidity can create. In addition, individuals should require a reasonable rate of return that is above and beyond that which is available from other more liquid options. Selling liquidity too cheaply is akin to being insufficiently insured. If things work out as planned the risk will be hidden from all but those with the knowledge to identify it. However, if things do not work out as planned the risk associated with illiquidity can be very damaging to a financial plan.

38

Roth vs. Traditional

When saving for retirement one of the first decisions that must be made is whether to contribute money to a Roth IRA/401(k) or a Traditional IRA/401(k). This is often framed as a tax decision as Roth and Traditional accounts have different tax treatment both in the year of the contribution and the year the money is withdrawn. However, there are other factors that should be considered which can have major implications when it comes to an individual's overall financial plan.

A Traditional account gives the saver a tax deduction in the year a contribution is made. In fact, this is one of the best tax deductions allowed under the tax code for several reasons. First, the taxpayer gets a tax deduction and gets to keep the money to grow it for their future. Other tax deductions, such as mortgage interest or charitable contributions, require the taxpayer to part with their money in order to get a percentage back in the form of a tax break. Second, contributions to Traditional accounts are subtracted from a taxpayer's Adjusted Gross Income (AGI) and Modified Adjusted Gross Income (MAGI). The level of a taxpayer's AGI and MAGI are used to determine whether the taxpayer will be eligible for certain other tax deductions and/or tax credits. Therefore, a deduction that lowers a taxpayer's

AGI and MAGI may have a double benefit as it will reduce their taxable income and could make them eligible for other deductions and/or credits which could further reduce their tax. Third, contributions to a Traditional account are not itemized deductions which must exceed the amount of the standard deduction to be beneficial. Therefore, even taxpayers with few other deductions may be able to lower their tax liability by contributing to a Traditional retirement plan.

The drawback of contributing to a Traditional retirement account is that when the money is withdrawn from the account it must be reported as income on the owner's tax return. Therefore, the amount accumulated in a traditional account may be whittled down to a smaller amount that can actually be spent after taxes are deducted.

A Roth account is basically the opposite of a Traditional account. The taxpayer does not receive a tax deduction in the year that the money is contributed but distributions are also not reported as taxable income when the money is withdrawn in retirement. Therefore, once the money is contributed to a Roth account the income and gains earned on the investments is essentially tax-free as long as the rules relating to qualified Roth distributions are followed. The Roth account may also offer the investor some additional flexibility. Subject to certain limitations Roth accounts may be used to fund the owner's or their dependent's education or medical expenses tax-free. In addition, the account owner may be able to use up to $10,000 from a Roth account to pay for a first-time home purchase without paying taxes on the withdrawal. This added flexibility can be valuable when planning for a home purchase or a dependent's education expenses.

The tax planning dilemma between a Traditional IRA/401(k) and a Roth IRA/401(k) largely comes down to the taxpayer's tax rate when the money is contributed compared to the tax rate when it is withdrawn in retirement. If the taxpayer is just starting to save for retirement and is subject to a low income tax rate, but expects their tax bracket to be higher in retirement, they may prefer a Roth account. This may allow them to prepay income taxes on the money at a low rate and withdrawal the money tax-free in retirement when they may be subject to a high tax rate. On the other hand, a taxpayer who is in their peak earnings years and is therefore subject to a high tax rate may prefer a Traditional account. This will allow them to claim a tax deduction when they are subject to the high tax rate and then pay taxes on the withdrawals in retirement when their tax rate may be lower. When the tax rate at the time of the contribution is the same as when the money is withdrawn there will be no tax advantage to one type of account over the other.

For example, if a taxpayer has $10,000 to invest and is subject to a 20% tax rate they can contribute the $10,000 to a traditional account with no tax due or pay $2,000 in income tax (20% of the $10,000) and contribute $8,000 to a Roth account. If the Roth account grows at a 10% rate for 10 years it will be worth $20,750 and can be withdrawn tax-free in retirement. If the Traditional account grows at the same rate over the same time period it would be worth $25,937 which will net the retiree $20,750 after $5,187 (20% of $25,937) in income tax is deducted.

However, taxes should not be the only consideration when choosing whether to contribute to a Roth or a Traditional account. Instead, the estimated tax savings based on the tax rate differential between the tax rate when the contribution is made and when the money is withdrawn should be weighed against other factors.

For example, contributing to a Traditional account may offer some protection against negative future events. If the account owner loses their job, and as a result their household's income falls, they may benefit from having more money saved due to the tax deduction allowed from contributing to a Traditional account. If the account owner is forced to withdrawal money from their retirement account it will be added to their income but the tax may be offset by tax deductions or taxed at a low rate due to the decrease in the taxpayer's income. On the other hand, the tax that was prepaid when the taxpayer made contributions to a Roth account cannot be recovered and therefore cannot be used to cover expenses until the taxpayer finds a new job. This access to additional funds can be even more important should the taxpayer die or become disabled. If the taxpayer is a major source of income for their household then the household income may fall to the level where withdrawals from a Traditional account are subject to little tax giving the household access to more money when it is needed most.

Next, money in a Traditional account may be converted to a Roth account at some point in the future whereas money in a Roth account cannot be shifted into a Traditional account. Therefore, a taxpayer who has volatile income can contribute to a Traditional account to get the tax deduction when their income and tax rate is high and then convert the money to a Roth account when their income is low allowing them to pay the taxes on the money at a lower rate. This can be an especially valuable strategy for years in which the taxpayer reports a business or real estate loss which can offset income from a Roth conversion. The ability to choose when to pay tax on retirement money can be a powerful planning tool which may allow a taxpayer to realize a tax benefit from a bad income year or poor investment taking some of the sting out of the loss of income or investment value.

Another potential benefit of contributing to a Traditional account is that the money may be tax-free (taxable income offset by deductions) when distributed if it is used to fund medical expenses or other tax-deductible expenses. For example, a certain percentage of taxpayers will need long-term health care services at some point in retirement. These services can be quite expensive and may be tax deductible which can lead to large tax deductions. In this case, money may be distributed from a Traditional account with little or no tax due. In addition, if the taxpayer has the goal of leaving money to charity they can use a Traditional IRA after they reach age 70.5 to fund charitable donations or they can name a charity as the beneficiary of all or a percentage of the account without ever incurring tax on the money.

Finally, a taxpayer should take into account their other sources of retirement income. If the taxpayer expects to have a large amount of taxable income in retirement from a pension or other sources they may benefit from having money in a Roth account so that they do not add to their taxable income in retirement. On the other hand, if the retirement account will be the primary source of retirement income then a Traditional account may be the better option as withdrawals will start at the lower tax bracket and work their way up so that the average tax rate may be fairly low. After all, when Traditional retirement account contributions are made they are deducted from income that would have been taxed at the taxpayer's higher tax rates but the withdrawals may fill up several tax brackets, some of which may be low and some higher. Therefore, to determine the potential savings the average estimated tax bracket for withdrawals should be compared to the taxpayer's highest tax brackets when the contributions are made.

At this point it may be clear that unless there is a substantial estimated tax benefit from contributing to a Roth account the greater flexibility and the tax deferral of the Traditional account may make it the superior option. However, there is one argument for Roth accounts that has not been covered. The argument is that the massive increase in the US national debt from $5.7 trillion in 2000 to over $21 trillion in 2018 combined with annual deficits of more than $1 trillion may necessitate higher income tax rates in the future. This may be valid thinking, or it may not. In the past it has been very difficult to forecast future income tax rates. After all, since 2000 there were major tax cuts in 2001 and 2017 all while the federal government's debt and deficits increased. So each individual investor will need to make their own estimate as to the risk of an increase in income tax rates.

Savers also have the option to hedge their risk of investing in one type of retirement account over the other by investing in both. Often there is the option of contributing half of retirement contributions to a Traditional account and half to a Roth account. This can be a good strategy when the pros and cons of each type of account appear to be balanced so that neither strategy is expected to outperform the other. Of course, it is recommended that individuals consult a financial planner before engaging in any financial decisions that cannot be easily and inexpensively reversed.

39

Tax Bracket Planning

Many people do not give their income taxes much thought until tax preparation season rolls around. Then they gather all of their tax forms, cross their fingers, and set up a meeting with their tax preparer or sit down at their computer to try to navigate through their tax preparation software. The problem with this strategy is that the majority of tax planning opportunities available to taxpayers must be implemented during the tax year. By the time tax season starts it is too late to make most of the changes that could reduce the amount of tax owed. In addition, this annual tax ritual creates a short-term focus on the tax owed for the year in question whereas longer-term planning may yield far greater savings. This means it can be more beneficial to plan to minimize taxes over the long-term even if it results in an increased amount owed in the short-term.

When engaging in long-term tax planning one of the most important factors to consider are the income levels at which a taxpayer will go into the next tax bracket. For example, a taxpayer may be in the 12% federal tax bracket and may be able to have $10,000 more in taxable income before they move into the 22% tax bracket. Given the substantial difference between the 12% tax bracket and the 22% bracket it may be beneficial to generate more income to prepay tax at the lower tax rate in order to reduce the risk of paying tax at the higher tax rate in the future. This type of planning may lead to a greater tax liability in the short-term, but it can reduce the taxpayer's average tax bracket over the long-term leading to long-term savings that exceed the short-term cost.

One way that tax bracket planning can benefit taxpayers is planning for large expenses. For example, retirees often take just enough money from their retirement accounts to fund their normal spending each year. But periodically retirees have a need for more income to fund a car purchase, a new roof for their home, or another large expenditure. This can cause them to bunch taxable income into years when they take larger withdrawals from retirement accounts to pay for unusual expenses. In some cases, these larger withdrawals can cause the taxpayer to enter the next tax bracket so that the income is taxed at a higher rate. However, this may be avoided if the taxpayer plans ahead. They may be able to take larger distributions from their retirement accounts in their lower income years in order to maximize the benefit of the lower tax bracket. The excess income can then be saved to pay for future expenditures.

Another way that tax bracket planning can benefit a taxpayer is to plan for required distributions from taxable retirement accounts. Many retirement accounts require that the owner withdraw a minimum amount each year beginning in the year they reach age 70.5. The percentage of the account that must be withdrawn and reported as income increases as the account owner ages. For some taxpayers this may push them into a higher tax bracket later in retirement than they were in earlier in retirement so that taxes take a big bite out of the required distributions. This risk can be managed by modeling the retiree's income and tax rates throughout their retirement and shifting income from high tax rate years to lower tax rate years. One way to do this is to strategically convert money from taxable retirement accounts to Roth accounts early in retirement when the tax rate is lower. This will reduce the balance in the taxable retirement accounts which will reduce the amounts that must be distributed after age 70.5. In addition, any investment returns in a Roth account will be tax-free rather than taxable which could further reduce future taxable income. By shifting income from projected high income tax rate years to low tax rate years the retiree can protect their investments from excess taxes and instead use the money to fund their future spending needs or preserve it for their beneficiaries.

When it comes to preserving retirement money for beneficiaries, tax bracket planning can take on a multigenerational approach. Often retirees hold investments that will pass taxable income to the next generation, such as taxable retirement accounts, annuities, and U.S. government savings bonds. In addition, a retiree may be in a lower income tax bracket than their beneficiaries who may still be working or may have accumulated substantial retirement resources of their own. In this case, the retiree may want to take more income from their taxable investments than they need in order to pay the tax at their lower tax rate. This will allow them to avoid passing those investments on to their beneficiaries who will likely pay a higher tax rate.

Finally, a tax bracket planning strategy can free up money that can be invested in assets that are best owned outside of retirement accounts, such as real estate, private loans, or a small business. This added flexibility may allow a retiree to achieve a greater level of investment diversification or take advantage of attractive investment opportunities which may not be available in retirement accounts. In this case, the higher investment returns or lower risk due to increased diversification may more than compensate for the taxes that were prepaid at the lower tax rate.

A tax bracket planning strategy should not be limited to retirees. Taxpayers who are still working may benefit from allocating their retirement savings to pretax and after-tax retirement accounts depending on the tax rate the income would be subject to. For example, assume a taxpayer wants to save $15,000 for retirement. Further assume that based on their income tax brackets $5,000 would be subject to the 22% tax bracket and $10,000 would be subject to the 12% tax bracket. The taxpayer could allocate $5,000 to a tax deferred retirement plan to avoid the high tax rate and $10,000 to a Roth 401k account. By allocating money between account types based on their tax brackets the taxpayer may be able to create a more tax efficient retirement savings strategy.

A tax bracket strategy can even be implemented when an individual does not pay income taxes. In some cases, an individual's income can be so low that their deductions more than offset their income leading to a negative taxable income. While paying no income tax may seem like a good thing, having a negative taxable income means the taxpayer could generate more income and still pay no income taxes. Sometimes this happens because of large medical expenses or a business or real estate loss during the tax year. In this case, it can be beneficial to try to generate income before the end of the tax year as it will be sheltered from income tax. If income cannot be pulled into the tax year the taxpayer should consider whether they can push some of the deductions into the next year where it may be able to offset future income. In general, reporting negative taxable income should be viewed as a lost opportunity to avoid paying taxes on additional income and should be avoided when possible.

One word of caution related to the Medicare premiums that many retirees pay out of their Social Security income. Medicare premiums are means-tested which means they increase after a taxpayer's income reaches a certain threshold. So, when engaging in a tax bracket planning strategy it is important to pay attention to the Medicare income thresholds to make sure they are not surpassed if it will lead to a smaller income tax benefit than the taxpayer will pay in additional Medicare premiums.

To be effective, a tax bracket planning strategy must be implemented before the end of a tax year and must take a long-term perspective. Ideally, such a strategy should be implemented early in the tax year and monitored periodically to make sure that any changes in income, deductions, or the tax law do not necessitate changes. While this may be more work, a strategy that seeks to minimize a taxpayer's tax liability over their lifetime rather than for a single year can result in substantial long-term tax savings.

40

Managing Tax Deductions

One of the most important parts of a taxpayer's income tax return is the type and amount of deductions they are able to claim. A taxpayer may choose to claim the standard deduction that is allowed for their filing status or they may choose to itemize their deductions. Naturally, it benefits the taxpayer to choose whichever deduction is greater in order to reduce their tax liability by as much as possible. However, with some preemptive planning and by taking a multi-year perspective a taxpayer may be able to get creative and gain an even greater benefit from their tax deductions.

For example, a common misconception is that it is better to itemize deductions rather than claim the standard deduction. This is not necessarily the case. Too often people keep a mortgage that they could pay off or make a charitable contribution because they value the income tax deduction. The problem is that itemized deductions cost money while the standard deduction is free. Therefore, taking the standard deduction can be advantageous from a financial standpoint even if it results in more income tax. For example, a taxpayer must pay mortgage interest to their mortgage lender to claim a deduction which means they are out the money paid. If they are in the 24% tax bracket they will only reduce their income taxes by 24 cents for every dollar paid in mortgage interest. In other words, they are paying 76% of their mortgage interest while the federal government is only subsidizing 24%. The same is true for charitable donations. If these expenses were not incurred the taxpayer's income tax bill may be higher but they would also have more money available to spend or save.

In some cases, the benefit that a taxpayer receives from their itemized deductions may be quite small. For example, assume that a married couple has $10,000 in deductions for state and local taxes, $8,000 for mortgage interest, and $7,000 for charitable deductions for a total of $25,000. The standard deduction for married taxpayers who file a joint return is $24,000 as of 2019. So only $1,000 of the itemized deductions actually benefit the taxpayers and $14,000 of the $15,000 in mortgage interest and charitable donations result in no tax benefit for federal taxes (state tax rules may differ). In this case, the taxpayers may be better off if they reduced their deductions to take the standard deduction and keep more of their money.

There may be opportunities for taxpayers to benefit from itemized deductions by alternating the years that they itemize. For example, an individual can make charitable contributions throughout the year and then make the contributions for the following year by year-end so that all the contributions are deductible in the current tax year. This will lump two years of charitable contributions into one year making the itemized deductions larger than normal to maximize the benefit in the years the taxpayer itemizes. Then in alternating years the taxpayer can claim the standard deduction when their itemized deductions are reduced. A similar strategy can be used with property taxes. In the years the taxpayer plans to itemize they can pay as much as possible in that year, assuming the $10,000 cap on state and local taxes does not limit the deduction. By doing this, the taxpayer may be able to shift a large portion of their charitable contributions and property tax deductions into every other year so that they have high itemized deductions in some years and low itemized deductions in other years when they will claim the standard deduction.

Finally, individuals may benefit from lumping their itemized deductions into years when they have large medical expenses which allow them to claim a medical deduction. For example, if a taxpayer needs expensive dental work they may want to also have any other medical procedures that require out-of-pocket payments in the same year. This will maximize the tax benefit for the medical payments and allow the taxpayer to get an even greater benefit from the other itemized deductions that were shifted into that same year.

Tax planning to maximize the savings from tax deductions can be an important part of a tax minimization strategy. This requires that taxpayers take a multi-year approach to tax planning and change their behavior in order to minimize their taxes. The key is to learn to take tax implications into account when making financial decisions in order to engage in preemptive planning rather than determining the tax implications afterwards when it cannot be changed. Such a strategy requires ongoing planning and monitoring but can result in substantial tax savings.

41

Retirement Savings Debt

Statistics show that Americans are not saving nearly enough for retirement. Some media sources have even labeled it a retirement savings crisis. With pension plans in decline, the household savings rate at low levels, and Social Security likely to only account for a portion of the income needed many people are ill prepared for retirement. While the current situation can be blamed on a variety of factors one of the major causes is people's attitudes about saving for retirement.

Most people do not know how much they need to save for retirement. In general, they know it is a big number but they also believe that retirement is a long way off. So they think of retirement savings like a long journey that they have plenty of time to complete. This often causes individuals to put off starting the journey. Others take baby steps toward retirement. After all, why commit money that can be spent today to a goal that is so far out in the future? Meanwhile, those who do save pat themselves on the back with each milestone passed: $10,000 saved, $25,000 saved, $50,000 saved and so on. While reaching these milestones is admirable, they may still be a long distance from the finish line. With the clock continually ticking weeks turn into months, months turn into years, and years turn into decades. Eventually, many people find themselves with too great a distance to travel and too little time to get there.

The outcome could be different if people had a different attitude about saving for retirement. Instead of viewing any savings as progress many people would benefit from viewing retirement savings as a debt that must be paid. After all, the money needed to fund retirement is like a debt that the present self owes to their future self. Just like a debt, the longer one delays making payments the greater the amount one will have to pay due to accrued interest. The longer one waits to start saving for retirement the more money that will have to come from saving and the less that will come from investment returns. Therefore, it is important to start early and make large enough payments to pay off the retirement savings debt by the desired retirement date.

When retirement savings is considered to be a debt, like a mortgage, it takes on a greater sense of urgency. If someone does not pay their mortgage they will lose their home. If they do not pay their retirement savings debt they will lose their opportunity for a comfortable retirement. In addition, making a mortgage payment may have tax benefits due to the deductibility of mortgage interest. Saving for retirement by contributing to a tax-deferred retirement account can also result in tax benefits. Finally, paying on a 30-year mortgage can feel daunting as the eventual payoff feels like it is a lifetime away. Saving for retirement requires a similar commitment as it often takes decades to accumulate a large enough sum to be able to fund a comfortable retirement which itself could last decades.

So what does it take to convert a retirement savings goal into a retirement savings debt? As with any debt it must be converted into a series of payments. To calculate the payment one needs to know the balance of the debt, the time period in which it must be paid, and the interest rate. For a retirement savings debt the balance is the amount of savings required to supplement other retirement income sources in order to maintain the retiree's standard of living in retirement. The time period is the time remaining until the retiree will reach their desired retirement age. The interest rate is the estimated annual rate of return for the payment period. The required savings amount, time period, and rate of return assumption can all be incorporated into a retirement projection to determine the monthly or annual payment required to meet the retirement savings goal.

If more people approached retirement savings like it were a debt that their younger self owes to their older self the retirement savings crisis may be averted. Debt payments require greater discipline than most people apply to retirement savings and can become a habit over time. A similar consistent long-term commitment is needed to accumulate sufficient savings to fund retirement.

42

Challenges to Early Retirement

Many people have the goal of retiring at a young age. While this goal may be possible with diligent savings, an intelligently designed financial plan, and some good fortune it is a lot more challenging than most realize. There are a number of factors that work against people who seek to retire early. Therefore, it is important to understand and incorporate these factors into a retirement plan.

The biggest challenge to retiring early is that it reduces the number of working years the individual has to save while increasing the number of retirement years they will have to fund. For example, an individual who starts working at age 20, expects to live until age 90, and plans to retire at age 65 will have 45 working years to fund 25 years of retirement spending. However, if the same individual wants to retire early at age 60 they will have just 40 years to save in order to fund 30 years of retirement spending. Retiring early does not simply require saving the amount needed to retire comfortably at age 65 by age 60. It requires saving more money in order to fund the additional years of retirement in less time.

This has two implications. The first is that the money has less time to grow so more must come from savings and less from investment returns. The second is that the reduced time to save and the increased savings target means much more money must be set aside each year. For an individual who starts saving for retirement early in their working years this could require saving a third more each year to retire at age 60 than it would have required to retire at age 65. Those who start saving later in their career may have to save as much as 50% more per year to retire early. Of course, the saving requirement will increase even more for someone who desires to retire even earlier than age 60.

In addition, the impact that retiring early has on Social Security benefits may need to be taken into consideration. An individual who retires at age 65 will likely receive a Social Security retirement benefit that is fairly close to their full retirement benefit. If they retire early they may be able to claim their retirement benefits as early as age 62 but the amount will be reduced. Therefore, an individual who retires early must save additional money to offset their reduction in Social Security benefits and cover any years before the benefits begin. For example, assume an individual's full Social Security benefit will be $1,500 per month. If they retire early and start taking benefits at age 62 they may only receive $1,200 per month. This $300 per month shortfall could require an additional $50,000 in retirement savings. In addition, if the individual retires at age 60 they may have two years before they can even draw Social Security benefits which must be covered by additional savings. This could add an additional $28,800 to retirement savings needs for a total of $78,800 in additional savings. If an individual wants to retire before age 60 the additional savings needed will be even greater.

Health insurance expenses are also a major cost for people who retire early. At age 65 many people are eligible to get health insurance though Medicare which is an affordable option for most. However, those who retire before age 65 may need to pay for private health insurance until they are eligible for Medicare. Since health insurance premiums increase as the insured ages the cost can be quite high, especially for those over age 60. As an example, an individual who retires at age 60 may need to have an additional $50,000 set aside to pay for private health insurance between age 60 and age 65.

Finally, when an individual retires early they have less time to pay off debts, such as their mortgage. Taking a mortgage into retirement can increase the retirement savings needed so that the mortgage can be paid off early or the payments can be made from savings. Depending on when the retiree takes out their last mortgage and the amount of the mortgage balance the additional cost may be a relatively small expense or a substantial amount that must be offset by additional savings.

These factors can combine to increase the amount that must be saved in order to retire early. In some cases, the additional savings amount can add up to several hundred thousand dollars. In addition, the earlier the retirement age the more that must be saved and the shorter the time period to save which may require substantial amounts to be set aside each year.

The good news is that the same factors that make it challenging for most people to retire early benefit those who choose to wait until age 65, or even later, to retire. This should be comforting to those who waited to start saving for retirement or feel that they are behind in saving for retirement as a few additional years working can make a big difference. When an individual delays retirement they not only have more years to save but they also need to fund fewer years of retirement spending. This means they have more years to set money aside and let their savings grow while their target savings amount is reduced due to the shortened retirement period.

Delaying retirement can also allow a retiree to delay taking their Social Security retirement benefits. When an individual waits to take Social Security benefits their monthly benefit is increased for every month they delay up until age 70. The larger Social Security benefit can further reduce the amount that needs to be saved for retirement. In some cases, pension benefits may also increase with the recipient's age having a similar effect as delaying Social Security benefits.

Obviously, not everyone wants to delay retirement. Therefore, it is important to create and implement a retirement plan as early as possible. Starting at a young age combined with disciplined saving and investing can make early retirement possible. However, it is important to start with reasonable expectations as to the savings rate required to achieve the goal.

43

Aggressively Saving for Retirement

According to recent data an increasing number of Americans have reported that they plan to work at least until age 65. However, in reality many of those who plan to work until age 65 may be forced into early retirement due to health issues, job loss, or some other unforeseen circumstances. When an individual is forced to retire early due to factors beyond their control they may be left with a retirement funding shortfall that results in reduced income and less financial security in retirement.

One of the major challenges for early retirees is the age gap that they may face before they are eligible for Social Security and Medicare. Social Security retirement benefits can be claimed as early as age 62. However, a worker that was planning to take Social Security at age 65 will receive a benefit that is approximately 20% less than planned if they begin their benefits at age 62. This could create a retirement income gap that will last for their lifetime, significantly reducing the total income available to fund retirement. In addition, the Medicare gap can add to expenses in the first years of retirement. An individual who is forced to retire at age 60 will have five years before they will be eligible for health insurance through Medicare. This can add as much as $50,000 of expenses to the first years of retirement forcing the retiree to draw down their retirement savings at a much faster pace than expected.

Fortunately, there are several ways for individuals to attempt to hedge the risks of a forced early retirement. One is to maintain adequate insurance. While long-term disability insurance can be quite expensive, it can be a key part of a retirement plan. Disability insurance payments may be used to fill the gap between earnings and retirement income should a major health issue force an individual to retire earlier than planned.

Another option is to aggressively save for retirement. For example, if the target retirement date is age 65, an individual may save as if they plan to retire at age 60. While this will require a higher savings rate, it will reduce the risk of falling short of achieving retirement goals should the retirement date come sooner than expected. Often, a savings surplus along with a severance package can allow an individual to bridge the gap between their target retirement date and their actual retirement date.

In addition, aggressively saving for retirement may give an employee the ability to take an early retirement package in which a company offers employees benefits to encourage them to retire rather than resorting to layoffs. Or an employee may be able to negotiate a customized severance package, for example a severance package that provides health insurance until Medicare age rather than cash compensation which may be subject to a high tax rate in the year of retirement.

Naturally, choosing to aggressively save for retirement can take a big bite out of a household's spending budget. However, even small amounts of additional savings can add up when funding long-term goals, such as retirement. For example, for those eligible, the Roth IRA can be a good supplemental savings vehicle as it can give an individual access to the money tax-free after age 59 1/2. An individual who saves $5,500 in a Roth IRA for 20 years earning an average annual return of 6% will have an additional $200,000. This money could be used to fill the funding gap from an early retirement. For many, this could be the difference between achieving their desired retirement lifestyle despite an early retirement and falling short of their goals.

The future is uncertain. This includes the stability of employment income, the rate of return earned on investments, the level of future tax rates, and many other factors that can impact retirement. Therefore, it may be advisable to err on the side of saving more than is needed to fund retirement to have the flexibility to adapt to any unexpected events.

44

Social Security

Social Security retirement benefits are a large portion of many people's retirement income. Yet the decision of when an individual should start drawing their benefits is the subject of debate. This is partially because many financial commentators approach their analysis using flawed calculations and logic. Too often, this leads to the one-sized-fits-all advice that does not take into account an individual's unique circumstances.

Social Security retirement benefits generally can be claimed as early as age 62. However, when an individual claims their benefits before their full retirement age the benefits will be reduced. On the other hand, the longer that a retiree delays claiming benefits the greater the amount that they will receive with benefits maxing out at age 70. Many financial commentators recommend that people delay taking their Social Security benefits until age 70 so that they get the maximum benefit available. This may be a good strategy for individuals who continue to work until age 70 or have sufficient income from a pension so that they do not need the income. But for many others the decision is far more nuanced.

To make an informed decision it is important to first understand the real benefit from delaying Social Security benefits. Every year that an individual delays drawing benefits their benefit amount increases by approximately 7%. However, when life expectancy statistics are applied one must assume that delaying benefits will mean that they will collect for a fewer number of years. For example, an individual that is age 65 may be expected to live on average 19 years until age 84. If they make the decision at age 65 to delay claiming benefits for one year they can expect to claim the higher benefit for just 18 years. Therefore, their expected lifetime benefits will not be 7% higher due to the fewer number of monthly checks.

Delaying Social Security benefits will result in a higher expected lifetime benefit. However, the percentage increase from delaying each year after life expectancies and future inflation rate assumptions are taken into account may be less than half of the 7% increase in monthly benefits. In fact, the estimated lifetime benefit from delaying Social Security retirement benefits by one year is approximately 3%. This number can be used to calculate what economists call the opportunity cost. Opportunity cost is the next best alternative to a financial decision. It is the option that is given up when a particular course of action is selected. If an individual chooses to draw their Social Security benefits before age 70 they are giving up the estimated increase in lifetime benefits, in this case the potential for a 3%+/- increase in Social Security benefits.

For example, assume an individual is in need of retirement income and has two options: Draw money out of a savings account at a bank earning 1% or start Social Security retirement benefits. In this case the estimated value of the Social Security benefits will increase approximately 3% per year while the money in the savings account will only increase at a 1% rate. Therefore, it may be advisable to draw the money needed from the bank account and delay taking Social Security benefits. On the other hand, if the question is whether to start Social Security benefits or draw money from an investment account with an expected annual rate of return of 6% it may be advisable to start Social Security benefits as the investment account is expected to produce a higher rate of return.

Of course, there are other considerations that should also be considered. If an individual has a history of longevity in their family and is in good health they may have good reason to believe that they will live longer than average. In this case, delaying Social Security retirement benefits may yield a greater benefit than 3% per year. However, there is also the risk that an individual's actual life expectancy may be shorter than average. If an individual spends down their assets in order to delay taking Social Security benefits and does not live long enough to realize the benefit from this strategy they will not be able to recoup the assets to their heirs or a surviving spouse. So the risk of spending down assets without realizing the benefit from delaying Social Security should be considered when planning a Social Security claiming strategy.

Tax implications should also be considered. The federal government does not fully tax Social Security retirement benefits and many states completely exclude these benefits from taxation. Therefore, it may be advantageous to take advantage of the lower tax rate on Social Security benefits rather than take money from a taxable retirement account which could push the retiree into a higher federal or state income tax bracket. Depending on the retiree's tax situation and other income sources the difference in tax liability may be substantial. In this case, drawing Social Security income rather than depleting retirement accounts may allow the retiree to reduce their tax liability by a large amount and therefore preserve more of their retirement resources for the future.

45

Mortgage Insights

A mortgage is often one of the largest financial commitments that an individual will make during their lifetime. Therefore, it is important to manage mortgage debt wisely by shopping for the best terms when the mortgage is originated, refinancing when interest rates decline enough to yield sufficient savings, and avoid cashing out home equity to fund consumer spending. However, there are also important behavioral and financial implications that should be considered when coordinating mortgage debt planning with retirement planning.

Paying off a mortgage can be a good way to bring retirement income and expenses into balance. When retirement income and expenses are out of balance there are two ways to solve the problem. The first is to work longer and save more in order to accumulate the additional savings required to produce the income needed. Research on sustainable withdrawal rates (the percentage of an account balance that can be withdrawn each year with a high statistical probability that the money will last) has shown that investors can expect to be able to draw approximately $1,000 in income per year for every $25,000 saved. Therefore, an individual with a $12,000 shortfall in retirement income will need an additional $300,000 in retirement assets to close the gap. On the other hand, if they have a mortgage with an annual payment of $12,000 and a balance of $100,000 they could close the gap by saving $100,000 to pay off their mortgage rather than saving $300,000 to invest for income. Often the strategy of paying off debt to reduce expenses rather than saving to invest and generate income can yield greater cash flow benefits and make it easier to bring income and expenses into balance.

Along this vein it should be noted that a common mistake many retirees make is choosing to keep a mortgage in retirement while investing after-tax money to generate income to make the payment. On the surface this seems like a good strategy as the average annual rate of return expected on the investments may be greater than the interest rate on the mortgage. However, the volatility of returns must also be considered. The rate of return on the investment portfolio is likely to vary from year to year with some years above the expected annual average return and some years below. In addition, some years the return may be negative so that the withdrawals combined with the investment losses will compound the drawdown in value. Meanwhile, the interest cost and mortgage payment will stay the same year after year. Therefore, if the investment markets experience a period of high volatility the value of the investments may decline at a faster rate than the mortgage balance leading to a loss of wealth.

This risk is demonstrated by the difference between the sustainable withdrawal rate for an investment portfolio and the mortgage payment as a percentage of the outstanding balance. For example, a new 30-year mortgage at a 4.5% interest rate will have a required payment (interest and principle) that is approximately 6% of the mortgage balance. As the mortgage balance is paid down over time the payment will remain the same so the payment as a percentage of the mortgage balance will increase. Meanwhile, if an amount equal to the mortgage balance is invested the sustainable withdrawal rate is only roughly 4%. Withdrawal rates of between 4% and 6% increase the risk that the investment portfolio will not be able to sustain the withdrawals and will decrease in value at a faster rate than the mortgage. When the withdrawal rate is above 6% there is a high probability that a period of even normal investment return volatility will put the account on an unsustainable path so that the account runs out of money before the mortgage is paid off.

This example shows that even though a financial planning strategy may have a higher average expected rate of return the risk of the strategy is important. Pairing variable returns with fixed costs can be a recipe for disaster. Therefore, this strategy should be avoided unless there are mitigating factors such as a high tax cost of accessing investments, a large amount of pension or Social Security income that can be used to pay the mortgage in years of poor investment returns, or the option of converting the mortgage to a reverse mortgage if the investment balance is unable to support the mortgage payments. However, in most cases it is advisable to pay off a mortgage at retirement to eliminate the liability and reduce the cash flow needed to fund retirement expenses.

If a mortgage cannot be paid off at retirement it may be advisable to refinance the mortgage in order to stretch out the payments as long as possible. This will reduce the minimum payment amount and thus the cash flow required to fund the mortgage payments. From a practical perspective it can be more valuable to increase the free cash flow early in retirement rather than later. Often retirees are most active in the first years of retirement because they finally have the time to do all the things they wanted to do, but did not have time to do, when they were working. A retiree that enters retirement with 10 years left on their mortgage may be stuck with large mortgage payments during those early retirement years and therefore have less financial flexibility to enjoy retirement. By stretching out the mortgage payments over a longer time period it can create more free cash flow to fund spending early in retirement.

So paying off a mortgage by retirement may be an ideal strategy. However, there is also a behavioral risk to paying off a mortgage before retirement. Eliminating the mortgage payment from household expenses can be a good thing from a financial perspective but it requires discipline or it could end up being a mistake from a behavioral perspective. Too often when a mortgage is paid off at least a portion of the household income that was dedicated to paying the mortgage payments is allocated to other expenses such as costlier vehicles, more expensive vacations, etc. To the extent that these expenses become a part of a household's standard of living they can increase the amount of income needed in retirement. Greater retirement income needs will increase the retirement assets that will be needed to produce retirement income. For example, a household that pays off a mortgage that had a payment of $2,500 per month will have an additional $30,000 per year of free cash flow. If this money is saved it can be a welcome addition to the financial resources used to fund retirement. However, if the money is spent and becomes a part of the household's standard of living it would require an additional $750,000 of retirement savings to generate the additional $30,000 per year of spending assuming a 4% sustainable withdrawal rate. In this case, paying off a mortgage before retirement can actually lead to a household moving further away from being able to retire at their desired retirement age unless they have the discipline to maintain their spending level and save the additional cash flow.

Mortgage planning is important both from a financial and a behavioral standpoint. The financial implications can be difficult to understand as the math required to do retirement scenario analysis can be complex. However, the behavioral implications often have an even greater impact on the final outcome. A competent financial planner can not only run retirement scenarios to test mortgage planning strategies but can also offer behavior coaching to avoid the common pitfalls of poor mortgage planning.

46

Planning for Cognitive Decline

N o one wants to think about a day when their mental faculties may decline to the point where they must rely on others. Unfortunately, with people living longer the odds that cognitive issues will become an issue during an individual's lifetime have increased. Therefore, it is important to have a contingency plan just in case cognitive impairment becomes a problem.

One common issue with many couples is that one spouse takes responsibility for financial tasks such as paying bills, managing investments, and monitoring their financial plan. This arrangement can work out well especially if one spouse takes an interest in finance while the other prefers to focus their efforts and attention elsewhere. A problem arises if the person that is focused on the finances suffers from cognitive impairment and is unable to continue to handle the responsibility. In this case, it is important to make sure the spouse is prepared to take over or else has a support network that can help them manage the finances. This is especially important for do-it-yourselfer investors and tax preparers who may not have a network of financial professionals who have access to their records, understand their financial situation, and have knowledge about their long-term financial goals and the strategies they are using to achieve them. The lack of an established network can leave the spouse, who may have limited financial knowledge, at the mercy of others who may not have the best intentions. Therefore, it may be beneficial to establish a network of trusted financial professionals that can step in to help with financial tasks as a backup plan.

It is also important to prepare an estate plan that addresses incapacity. An estate plan typically incudes a trust, a financial power of attorney, and a health care power of attorney. These documents name a successor trustee and an agent that can act on an individual's behalf should they become unable to make their own decisions. The person named as the successor trustee and agent should be considered carefully as this person should be aware of the individual's desires and be knowledgeable about financial matters or have access to well-qualified advisors. If there is no one that meets these criteria there are professionals who act as private fiduciaries which often have an extensive network of vetted financial professionals that they can call on when needed.

When preparing an estate plan it is important to pay close attention to the definition of incapacity used in the documents. Most people prefer to keep their incapacity a private matter by avoiding the courts and instead allowing their physicians to make a determination of their cognitive abilities. If this is the case, then it is important that the definition of incapacity in the estate planning documents reflect this desire. It is also important to understand the requirements of the financial institutions, tax authorities, and other financial intermediaries that will need to accept the estate planning documents and proof of incapacity.

Finally, it is important to maintain accurate and detailed financial records. Many people have a financial system that works for them. However, it is just as important that the system be easy for someone else to figure out in case they must take over. Too often bills go unpaid, investments are unaccounted for, and tax records are missing when an individual becomes incapacitated. This can lead to serious financial issues which may or may not be resolved depending on the records that are available and how they are organized.

47

Who Gets What

Most people do not want to think about their own mortality. For this reason, end of life planning is often neglected which is why far too few people have a financial plan that covers the risk of their own incapacity or death. Even those who have addressed this risk by creating a trust, establishing a financial and health care power of attorney, and completing beneficiary designations for their retirement accounts and insurance policies do so with little thought as to how their assets may be passed to their heirs most efficiently. This can lead to higher taxes, reduced flexibility for their heirs, and lost opportunities to achieve financial goals in a more efficient manner.

When it comes to estate planning there are two primary categories of assets: Those that will pass on taxable income to the heirs and those that will not. Some investments, such as tax-deferred retirement accounts, annuities, and US savings bonds, are often taxable to the beneficiaries after the owner's death. Other assets, such as non-retirement accounts, real estate, Roth accounts, and collectables, may receive a step-up in basis so that the beneficiary is treated as though they purchased the asset for its fair market value on the owner's date of death. This can lead to little or no tax consequences if the asset is sold soon after the original owner's death.

Obviously, most beneficiaries would prefer to inherit assets that are tax-free rather than taxable. However, different beneficiaries may have different tax situations so that one beneficiary's tax aversion is greater or lesser than another. In addition, some beneficiaries, such as a qualified charity, may not be subject to income taxes making them indifferent as to whether they receive assets that are taxable or tax-free. Yet too often this distinction is ignored when creating a plan to distribute assets after an individual has died.

For example, assume an individual would like to pass 10% of their assets to a qualified charity at their death and then have the remainder split between their two children, one in a high tax bracket and one in a low tax bracket. If all their assets are divided according to this formula the charity will receive 10% of their tax-free assets even though the charity is not subject to income tax. In addition, the child in a high tax bracket will receive 45% of the taxable assets making the tax authorities a sizable beneficiary of the assets as well.

What if a different approach was taken? For example, what if the charitable bequest was funded entirely from taxable assets? These assets would avoid taxation entirely and would leave more tax-free assets available to the children. In addition, tax-free assets could be first allocated to the decedent's child that is in a high tax bracket with a greater amount of taxable assets allocated to the child in the lower tax bracket to further reduce the taxes paid. Even if more money is allocated to the child in a lower tax bracket to compensate for the taxes both beneficiaries will be better off on an after-tax basis.

It may also be beneficial to pass taxable assets to younger beneficiaries, such as grandchildren. Not only might younger beneficiaries be in a lower tax bracket, but they may also be able to stretch out the taxable income over a greater number of years to benefit from a longer period of tax-deferred growth. Younger beneficiaries may also be able to increase the amount they are contributing to a tax-deferred retirement plan thereby creating a tax deduction that may offset any taxable income from their inheritance. This strategy could keep the money sheltered from tax and hopefully growing for generations.

Taxation may not be the only factor that should be considered. Sometimes control of the assets and the manner they are distributed after death may also be important. For example, if a beneficiary cannot be trusted to manage their own finances or if the assets would become subject to the claims of creditors it may be better to leave the assets to an irrevocable trust for the beneficiary's benefit. This will allow control of when and how the money is paid out after death. However, irrevocable trusts can be subject to high tax rates creating a tradeoff between tax efficiency and control. This may be mitigated by allocating tax-free assets to the trust in an effort to keep the trust's taxable income and tax rate as low as possible.

Finally, it is important to think about the character of an asset and if it will be more valuable under a certain beneficiary's control. For example, if the list of assets includes real estate, and one beneficiary is knowledgeable about real estate, it may be more valuable under their control without other less knowledgeable owners to deal with. In addition, if one beneficiary is involved in the operations of a small business or family farm those assets may be best left to them as they may be in the best position to derive value from those assets.

Choosing a tax efficient, value maximization approach to beneficiary designations and other forms of after-death asset distribution may be a superior strategy to the typical strategy of distributing all assets according to the same formula. While this strategy may require more forethought, planning, and monitoring it can make a big impact on the long-term value that is derived by the beneficiaries.

48

Skin in the Game

I n the financial world conflicts of interest are a common issue. In some cases, they are a part of the normal functioning of the financial system. For example, if investor A believes that a bond he holds will go down in value he may seek to sell it. If investor B believes the bond will increase in value she may be willing to buy it. It is in investor A's interest to have the bond go down in value making the trade a smart move while it is in investor B's interest to have the bond go up in value to produce a profit. This conflict of interest must exist for a transition to take place. If the interest of both investors were aligned so that they both wanted an asset to increase or decrease in value then no transaction would take place and no price would be assigned to the asset in question. This type of conflict of interest is a good thing because both investors have skin in the game and are clear about their intentions. In this case, skin in the game means they will participate in the gain or loss that results from their actions.

A problem occurs when a third party is introduced who does not have skin in the game. For example, assume investor A is very knowledgeable about the bond he owns and believes it will decrease in value. So he contacts an investment banker to help him sell it in exchange for a commission. The investment banker then contacts investors B, who is not very knowledgeable about the bond, and recommends that she purchase it. The fact that the investment banker does not have skin in the game (will not incur a profit or loss based on the performance of the bond) should make investor B very leery of relying on the investment banker's recommendation. Anyone with a lack of skin in the game should be viewed with a healthy dose of skepticism.

Unfortunately, the list of financial market participants that do not have skin in the game is quite long. First among these are the many purveyors of investment newsletters promoting hot stock tips, options trading strategies, or ways to profit from an impending economic boom or bust. These marketers are compensated in the form of newsletter subscription fees which do not change depending on the value of the newsletter content. If a newsletter gets bad reviews due to poor advice it is too easy to set up a new website and rebrand the newsletter to start fresh.

Many financial advisors also do not have skin in the game. Those who receive compensation, such as a sales commission, that is not impacted by the performance of the investments they recommend, or who recommend investments that they themselves to not own, do not have skin in the game. Therefore, their recommendations should be scrutinized to make sure their advice is not tainted by conflicts of interest. In addition, some advisors move from firm to firm regularly because they have no investment in the ownership or reputation of the investment companies they work for. Such a free agent is able to move on from client to client and firm to firm with impunity, the ultimate example of a professional with no skin in the game.

In the financial world there is nothing more unjust than a financial advisor or their firm profiting while their clients lose their hard-earned money. Yet this has been far too common. In the past few decades it has come to light that financial analysts recommended technology stocks that they knew were of little value, investment bankers advised pension funds to purchase mortgage backed bonds that they knew were expected to default, and credit rating analysts assigning their highest credit score to bonds that were likely to default. What did all of these cases have in common? The perpetrators had no skin in the game.

For this reason, it is important to recognize when someone has skin in the game and when they do not. A financial advisor that has an ownership stake in their firm, receives compensation that is tied to their client's success or failure, and personally owns the investments they recommend has skin in the game. This does not mean the advisor will always advocate the right strategy as no one is infallible but it is a way to minimize or avoid many conflicts of interest.

49

Trust but Verify

Economic and financial interactions are largely based on trust. In the developed world there are complex legal systems that can be used to resolve disputes. However, going through the courts can be costly and time consuming making it a last resort. Instcad, people count on trust to stay out of the courts and keep transaction costs low. So, despite the legal and regulatory protections in place, trust remains the cornerstone upon which modern society is built.

While trust is important, former President Ronald Regan had a saying that is good advice for everyone: "Trust but verify." In today's world of specialization it is impossible to be knowledgeable about everything. Complex fields like health care, finance, real estate, etc. require working with experts which requires a degree of trust. However, it is important to verify the work of those experts.

In finance, verification can take several forms. For example, it is important to review tax returns carefully to confirm that the information is accurate. Using a professional tax preparer is advisable given the complexity of the tax code and the work that is required to keep up with changes in the law. However, the taxpayer must sign the return attesting to the accuracy of the information it contains because the taxpayer will be held responsible by the tax authorities.

In addition, it is important to put checks and balances in place when monitoring investment accounts. Many investment custodians provide their customers with statements but these statements typically only list investment values and transactions. To supplement these statements investment managers should provide their clients with investment reports that list the asset allocation and rates of return. It is important that both are provided as the statements can be used to check the information on the investment report. This way no one person or single firm has control over all the information making it very difficult for an individual or a small group of collaborators to falsify investment values and returns.

It is also important to verify that an estate plan contains the proper language and provisions to accomplish an individual's goals. Typically, the creation of an estate plan starts with an individual or couple meeting with an estate planning attorney to discuss their goals. Then the attorney drafts the required documents which are delivered to the client for signing. Too often the client never actually reads the documents to confirm that they accurately reflect their goals. In some cases, the client only discovers the errors years later when they are in the process of updating their estate plan. In other cases, the discrepancies are not discovered until it is too late. If the technical language contained in the documents makes them difficult to decipher an individual should ask their financial planner or other advisor to review and summarize the estate plan to ensure that everything is in order.

Risk management is another area where "trust but verify" applies. Too often people are surprised by the terms and limits of their insurance policies when it comes time to file a claim. Many insurance companies choose to compete with one another based on price. This encourages them to offer minimal coverage in order to keep their prices (premiums) low. While these coverage limits may meet the minimums required by law, they may not be sufficient to adequately manage the policyholder's risk. For this reason, it is important for policyholders to verify their policy limits and any terms and conditions which could leave them exposed to large financial losses.

Finally, retirement plans should be verified. Retirement planning is often a central part of an overall financial plan. Unfortunately, some retirement plans use basic assumptions and a one-size-fits-all approach based on limited information to draw conclusions about an individual's retirement readiness. Should the assumptions prove to be faulty, or the information used insufficient, the conclusions may be invalid. Therefore, it is important to verify that a retirement plan is based on reasonable assumptions and uses sufficiently rigorous statistical methods to test its conclusions before relying on it.

Often financial planners can help their clients to verify that their taxes, investments, insurance, and other aspects of their finances fit their goals and objectives. Financial planners are in a unique position, given their knowledge of many financial disciplines and understanding of their clients overall financial picture, to offer a second opinion about many financial topics.

50

Hire a Financial Planner

Many people benefit from working with a financial planner. A competent financial planner will be knowledgeable about investments, taxes, retirement planning, insurance, employee benefits, estate planning, education funding, and budgeting. They will also have the skill required to pull all these areas together into a comprehensive financial plan. This knowledge is not possessed by most people who do not work in the financial industry and can be very valuable in a society where financial matters have become increasingly complex.

A financial planner's knowledge and expertise can help their clients avoid financial mistakes and take advantage of opportunities that otherwise may have been missed. One way a financial planner can do this is by correcting unrealistic assumptions. Too often people make financial plans that appear reasonable on the surface but when the assumptions are reviewed it becomes clear that the plan is unlikely to work out as expected. Financial planners can also benefit their clients by correcting misconceptions about the laws and regulations related to financial activities. Laws and regulations are constantly evolving which can make it difficult for the public to keep up with the many changes.

A financial planner can help their clients avoid unknowingly running afoul of the rules by catching potential problems ahead of time. A financial planner may also be a great source of financial education that is focused on an individual's unique financial situation. This way the individual does not have to spend hours on general financial education which is likely to include many aspects that do not relate to their individual situation.

Obviously, there are costs to hiring a financial planner as the planner will need to be compensated for their time and expertise. Many view this as a drain on an individual's financial resources and argue that expenses should be minimized as much as possible. While fees and expenses are an important issue that should be considered carefully it is also important to consider the benefits that an individual may receive from working with a financial planner. These benefits come in several forms. The first is the value of the time that a financial planner can save their clients. Monitoring financial markets, keeping up with changes in tax and financial laws, and creating and monitoring financial plans all require a substantial time commitment. Hiring a financial planner can relieve an individual of these responsibilities as they can delegate a large portion of the work. Second, working with a financial planner may allow an individual to avoid making a big financial mistake. Often, one poor decision can set an individual back years or even decades financially. Therefore, the value of having a planner reviewing financial decisions and offering feedback can be tremendous. Naturally, these benefits do not accrue year after year. There may only be one or two times over an individual's lifetime where a mistake is avoided due to access to professional advice. Yet the benefits that can be derived may be large enough to justify a lifetime of fees paid to a financial planner. Third, financial planners are often able to use their position in the financial services industry to get their clients access to lower cost investment and services options. Many of these services are either not available to do-it-yourself financial planners or are only available at much higher costs. Meanwhile, a planner can access resources by paying one fee and using it for all their clients, spreading out the cost across hundreds of financial planning engagements, rather than each client paying the full cost individually.

The value of working with a financial planner is not limited to the planner's knowledge of complex financial issues. Financial issues often have an emotional component which can cloud the judgement of even the most rational decision maker. When faced with an emotional financial decision it can be important to have a trusted third party review the decision from a knowledgeable outsider's perspective. In some cases, the second opinion can prevent an individual from making a terrible financial mistake based on emotion rather than rationally weighing the costs and benefits. In other cases, an impartial financial planner may support the decision allowing the individual to move forward with confidence rather than worrying that they might have made a big mistake.

Since no one can think objectively about their own finances the emotional aspects of decisions will often influence their choices, sometimes in a positive way and sometimes in a negative way. This is true no matter how much knowledge or experience an individual has in financial matters. The emotional influence can create blind spots to risks that should be avoided. It may also cause individuals to inflate their expectations for the benefits of a decision in order to justify the choice they want to make whereas more reasonable expectations would lead to the opposite conclusion. In addition, when an individual wants to support a given choice they often succumb to confirmation bias in which they seek out data that supports their preference while ignoring evidence that contradicts their preferred choice. A knowledgeable outsider can point out such biases by bringing contradictory data to the forefront and having a constructive discussion about the pros and cons of a decision. For this reason, everyone can benefit from working with a financial planner, even those who are financial planners themselves.

Appendix 1

The most commonly used financial statement is the balance sheet. A balance sheet consists of two columns: Assets are listed in the left column and liabilities are listed in the right column. Assets are everything that an individual owns that has a value. Liabilities are everything that the individual owes. The bottom of a balance sheet lists net worth which is the value of all the assets in the left column minus the value of all the liabilities in the right column. Net worth is a measure of an individual's total financial wealth. If the liabilities listed on the balance sheet are greater than the total value of the assets the net worth will be negative. This means that even if all of the assets were sold there would not be enough money to pay off all of the debts.

Net worth is important because it is the true measure of financial progress. Many investors focus only on the assets that they own. They fail to take into consideration the effect that increasing liabilities have on their financial wellbeing. This can lead to a false sense of financial progress. Net worth factors in both assets and liabilities to create a more accurate financial assessment. For this reason individuals should use net worth as the basis for their long-term goals which makes the balance sheet an important document when tracking progress.

Assets are generally divided into at least three categories. These are current assets, investment assets, and personal use assets. Current assets are those which are currently liquid or can be liquidated within one year. A liquid asset is one that is or can be converted to cash quickly without a loss of value or paying substantial fees. Examples of current assets are cash, money market accounts, checking accounts, and certificates of deposit (CD) of one year or less.

Investment assets are assets that are committed for a period longer than a year with the objective being appreciation in value or to generate income. Stocks, bonds, real estate, and certificates of deposit with a maturity of longer than one year are all examples of investment assets.

Personal use assets are the real property that is used in day-to-day life. This property has a value that typically decreases over time. It can be sold and converted to cash but often only at a deep discount to its fair value. Examples of personal use assets are furniture, vehicles, and clothing. A home can be an investment asset as opposed to a personal use asset because it will likely appreciate in value over time and may be sold in the future. However, if the home will not be sold to fund other financial goals it should be considered a personal asset. Jewelry or artwork can be either a personal asset or investment asset depending on the likelihood of price appreciation and whether it will be sold in the future. Within these categories assets are normally listed in order of liquidity with the most liquid assets listed first and the least liquid assets listed last.

Liabilities are typically divided into at least two categories: Current liabilities and long-term liabilities. Current liabilities are debts that are required to be paid within one year or less. Long-term liabilities are debts that are required to be paid later than one year. For example, a 30-year mortgage loan is a long-term liability until its last year (the 30th year) when it becomes a current liability. Revolving lines of credit such as credit card debts are current liabilities because they have no set term.

Statement of Change in Net Worth:

One of the drawbacks of the balance sheet is that it is an inventory of assets and liabilities as of a specific date. To track financial progress over time requires a statement of change in net worth. This is a financial statement that compares the differences between the current balance sheet and one that was created previously.

A statement of change in net worth lists the percentage of change in assets, liabilities, and net worth from one period to another. It will allow an individual to identify the percentage increase or decrease in their assets or liabilities that have occurred during the period and help them to see the effect that these changes had on their net worth. Tracking the percentage of change in net worth is a great way to get an overall indication of financial progress over time. Generally, the goal is to have an increasing net worth. However, in practice the net worth may actually decline from time to time.

If the net worth is declining, remaining the same, or not growing as quickly as one would like a statement of change in net worth can often show why this is. Reviewing the percentage change in the different categories of assets and liabilities can highlight areas of the balance sheet where progress is being made as well as the problem areas that are eroding net worth. Problems areas may include assets that have fallen in value by a substantial amount or liabilities that have increased dramatically. Identifying these problem areas is the first step to improving the balance sheet. The next step is to use the two financial statements listed next to find the cause of the less than desired results.

Income and Expense Statement:

When most people think of budgeting they are actually thinking of an Income and Expense Statement. This is a financial statement that tracks and categorizes sources of income and expenses. Creating an income and expense statement is the best way to track day-to-day financial transactions.

An Income and Expense Statement covers a period of time, typically one month or one year, as opposed to being as of a single date like a balance sheet. It categorizes and lists all of the financial transactions that occur during that time period. The benefits of creating an income and expense statement are that it shows where the income comes from and how it is being spent. By using categories one can lump sources of income and similar expenses together to make the information easier to digest.

To create an Income and Expense Statement one must list all income by sources. Common sources of income are wages, retirement funds, investments, Social Security benefits, or gifts. The income from all of these sources represents the total income for the period. The total after-tax income less the amount set aside for savings or investment is the net income for the period.

Expenses can be broken down into three major categories under which there may be several customized subcategories. These major categories are fixed expenses, variable expenses, and discretionary expenses. Fixed expenses are the expenses that are always the same amount or increase every year by a small amount which can be anticipated with fairly reasonable accuracy. Examples are a car payment, property taxes, and most insurance premiums. Variable expenses are those that change from month to month and include all necessities that are not fixed expenses. Variable expenses may change because the amount billed depends on usage or because of changes in behavior. Examples include an electric bill, gasoline costs, and expenditures on food. The third major category of expenses is discretionary expenses. These come out of discretionary income which is net income minus all necessary expenses. Discretionary expenses are those that an individual has the most control over. They represent wants, not needs. If an individual finds that they are having a hard time saving they should first look for discretionary expenses that can be reduced or eliminated. On the other hand, if one finds that they have income left over after subtracting discretionary expenses from discretionary income they should increase the amount that they save or invest each month.

Cash Flow Statement:

A cash flow statement is a simplified way of tracking the cash that is coming in and going out. In this respect it is similar to an income and expense statement except that is puts income and expenses together in three major categories. A cash flow statement is also unique in that it allows an individual to track the money that comes in as a result of borrowing where an income and expense statement does not. The three major categories of a cash flow statement are operational cash flows, investment cash flows, and financing cash flows.

The first category, operational cash flows, includes all income from working and cash out flows for normal living expenses as well as the purchase and upkeep of personal property. Businesses track operational cash flow to determine their profit or loss derived from normal business activities. For an individual, operational cash flows are the net income or net expense from daily living. If an individual is in their working years their operational cash flow should be positive. This means that more income is coming in than expenses going out. If an individual is retired or unemployed their operational cash flow may be negative as they are likely living on their savings or borrowing to pay living expenses.

Investment cash flow is all investment income such as interest earned on a savings account, interest payments on a bond investment, and stock dividends less any new investment purchases. This category displays the change in investment earning power as assets are accumulated. When an individual is young their investment cash flow should be negative. This is because they should be adding money to purchase investments which will start out small and generate little income. As they age their investment assets will increase and will likely be transitioned into income producing assets like bonds and high dividend paying stocks as they get closer to retirement. By middle age investment cash flows will likely be even as the investment income produced increases to the point that it equals the investment contributions. During retirement years investment cash flow will likely be positive as contributions are no longer made and the asset selection will strongly favor assets that generate income. Often during retirement the positive investment cash flow is used to offset a negative operational cash flow.

Financing cash flow is all cash inflows and outflows that are a result of borrowing. Inflows occur when money is borrowed and outflows occur when payments are made. In a given year financing cash flow may be a positive number as money is borrowed to purchase a house or a car. However, financing cash flow should typically be negative which means that debt is being paid off. If financing cash flow is positive on a regular basis it can be a red flag, especially if operational cash flows are negative. This means that an individual is borrowing to pay for living expenses which is not sustainable over the long-term.

About the Author

Chase Armer is a co-owner of Planned Solutions, Inc., a Sacramento based Financial Planning and Investment Advisory Firm where he works as a financial planner and is a member of Planned Solution's Investment Management Committee.

Chase holds several professional designations including: CERTIFIED FINANCIAL PLANNER™, Chartered Financial Analyst®, and Enrolled Agent. Chase has earned a Doctorate in Business Administration and a Masters in Taxation from William Howard Taft University, a BA in Economics from California State University, Sacramento, and a Certificate in Personal Financial Planning from the University of California at Davis Extension.

Chase is active with the Financial Planning Association of Northern California where he has served as President and the Director of Career Development. Chase has over 20 years of experience in the financial services industry, working primarily with individuals and business owners who seek advice in all areas of financial planning with a special emphasis on Investments, Retirement Planning, and Income Taxation.

Chase Armer can be contacted at:

Planned Solutions, Inc.
1130 Iron Point Road, Suite 170
Folsom, CA 95630
Tel. 916-361-0100
Fax. 916-361-0191
CArmer@PlannedSolutions.com